The
Thames Path

National Trail Companion

8th edition published February 2013

© National Trails Office

ISBN 978-0-9561074-4-2

Edited by Jos Joslin and Elaine Townson

Published by
National Trails Office
Signal Court, Old Station Way
Eynsham OX29 4TL

tel 01865 810224
email Nationaltrails@oxfordshire.gov.uk
website www.nationaltrail.co.uk

Designed by Linda Francis
tel 01865 407626

Cover photograph by Jos Joslin:
The River Thames at Eysey, downstream of Cricklade

Contents

Introduction

The Thames Path follows England's best known river for 184 miles (294 km) as it meanders from its source in Gloucestershire through several rural counties and on into the bustle of the City of London. On its way the Path passes peaceful water meadows rich in wildlife, historic towns and many lovely villages, finishing at the Thames Barrier in Woolwich. Easy to reach by public transport, this National Trail can be enjoyed in many ways, whether for an afternoon's stroll, a weekend's break or a full scale, but relatively gentle, trek of its whole length.

Welcome to the Thames Path Companion. It provides up-to-date practical information about accommodation, refreshments and many other facilities along the 294 km (184 miles) of National Trail from the source of the river in Gloucestershire, through Wiltshire, Oxfordshire, Berkshire, Buckinghamshire, Surrey and into London. The Companion is designed to help with planning anything from a three week's walking holiday to an afternoon out with the dog.

The Companion is not a route guide: for detailed information of the Trail itself, **The Thames Path National Trail Guides** are available from most book shops. Alternatively they can be mail ordered from the National Trails Office (see page 16 for details). The Companion complements the Trail Guides and, armed with a copy of each, it is hoped that anyone using the Trail needn't require anything more. Enjoy your trip.

Opened in 1996 as one of thirteen National Trails in England, the Thames Path follows the country's best known river as it meanders from its source in the Cotswolds through several rural counties and on into the heart of London. This Trail provides level, easy walking and can be enjoyed in many ways, whether for an afternoon's stroll, a weekend's break or a full scale, but relatively gentle trek of its whole length. Another advantage is that the Thames Path can be easily reached by public transport, including an excellent network of train services the whole distance between Oxford and London.

At the start of the Path, the source of the River Thames beneath an elderly ash tree in a field in the Cotswolds, you may well find no water at all. However, gradually as you travel the trickle becomes a stream and soon a river bordered by willows and alders. As far as Oxford, apart from a couple of small historic towns and a few pleasant villages, there is a real sense of remoteness and rural tranquillity as the Thames winds its way through flat water meadows grazed by cattle or sheep, or fields of crops.

Beyond Oxford, the city of dreaming spires, you will still be in the heart of the countryside with its wealth of wildlife. The river whose banks you're following continues to widen, the willows seem to grow larger, and settlements become more frequent. From

I INTRODUCTION

Goring where the Path coincides for a short distance with another National Trail, the ancient Ridgeway, the Chiltern Hills provide a wooded backdrop to your journey with their colours changing dramatically with the seasons.

When you reach Henley the Path starts to get busier with more people enjoying strolls with a dog, picnics on the bank or boating trips on the water. However, once you're away from towns or villages around a bend or two of the river, you'll regain the rural peacefulness. As the Thames Path passes beneath Windsor Castle, you are reminded that you are following a Royal river; the palaces of Hampton Court and Kew a little further downstream confirm this.

From the last non-tidal lock on the Thames at Teddington, you can choose to walk on either the north or the south bank of the river through most of London. You'll pass leafy Richmond and Kew, remarkably green areas, before entering the heart of the City with its many famous buildings bordering the Thames. The final few miles to the finish at the Thames Barrier take you amongst restored warehouses and the working wharves in London's Docklands.

With the support of Natural England, the Thames Path is managed, by the local highway authorities with a small dedicated team of National Trails staff and volunteers, to the highest standards necessary for one of the most important long-distance paths in the country.

Radcot Bridge

The Thames Valley was originally settled by prehistoric people with the earliest occupations discovered so far dating from the New Stone Age, some 6 000 years ago. These are at Runnymede and Staines near the Thames, not far from present day London. The river has been a very important trading route for hundreds of years and it was only during the latter half of the twentieth century that it mostly ceased to carry goods. Nowadays leisure boats rather than barges are the main users of the Thames.

It was in medieval times that the river became increasingly important for trade, especially in those days for carrying wool from the lush Cotswold meadows to London. St Paul's Cathedral is built of Taynton stone quarried in the Cotswolds and carried to London by barges towed by men and horses from Radcot. By the 18th century London was the world's busiest port and Reading, for example, received 95% of its goods by barge towed along the River Thames.

The towpath between Lechlade and Putney, along which much of the Thames Path now travels, was established towards the end of the 18th century by the Thames Commissioners at a time when the country's new canal system was being built which connected the Thames to other parts of Britain. It was a difficult task since many landowners refused permission for the towing path to enter their land or there were natural obstacles in its way. As a result in many places the towpath switched from one bank of the river to the other and ferries were used to transfer the towing horses across the river. When the commercial traffic died as a result of competition from the railways so did the navigation ferries.

This created a major problem for the setting up of the Thames Path. Either bridges had to be built where the old ferries used to operate or alternative routes to the towpath had to be found.

III WILDLIFE

Wherever you walk along the Thames Path there should be plenty of wildlife to observe and enjoy although, of course, the time of year you are there is important. There will be birds present all year round, but if you're keen on wild flowers then April to September is the time to visit, and if insects are an interest of yours choose June to September.

Plants of the riverside seem to be especially colourful from the bright yellow of the flag iris and marsh marigold in spring to the pinks of the willowherbs and purple loosestrife during summer. Plants of particular note along the Path are the nationally rare Loddon lily and snakeshead fritillary, both flowering on a few flood meadows in early spring.

Insects are in abundance during the summer when dragonflies and damselflies, amongst the largest and so most noticeable, are active. There are various species, many wonderfully coloured, and you'll be able to watch them mating, laying eggs, hunting for food or patrolling their territories.

Snakeshead fritillaries

Of the mammals you'll no doubt see rabbits and maybe a stoat or a weasel. Unfortunately you're unlikely to see an otter, a relative of the latter, although thankfully they are returning to the upper reaches of the Thames and perhaps in the future will be more plentiful and obvious. Another animal in trouble is the water vole, 'Ratty' of Kenneth Grahame's 'Wind in the Willows'. They used to be very common on the Thames emerging from their holes in the bank and busily ploughing backwards and forwards across the river, but their numbers have crashed in recent years. Let us know if and where you spot one.

The most obvious animals are the birds, many of which being water birds are large and thankfully don't fly away as soon as you appear! The majestic mute swan has to be the symbol of the Thames and is increasingly common thanks to the ban in the 1980s on anglers using lead weights. Swans eating these weights in mistake for the grit they need to take in to break down plant material in their gizzards were poisoned and killed and their numbers diminished considerably.

Wherever you go you'll see the commonest of Britain's ducks, the mallard, which like all ducks is especially resplendent from October to March. But other species of ducks visit the river too, so look out for tufted duck, pochard and wigeon. Geese, larger relatives of ducks, also abound in places, usually found in large noisy flocks grazing in fields near the river or roosting on the water itself. The Canada goose is very common.

Mute swan

IV PREPARING FOR YOUR VISIT

The Thames Path is primarily a route for use by walkers, although in a few places, especially in towns and cities and near London, cyclists can use sections. In a few places horseriders, too, can share the Path.

Spring, summer and autumn months are the best time to enjoy the Thames Path since there is very little risk of the river flooding and making the Trail impassable.

Deciding where to start

The Thames Path can be walked in either direction and is signposted both ways. The route is generally promoted from west to east, starting at the source and finishing at the Thames Barrier, because prevailing winds tend to come from the southwest and so will be mostly behind you.

How far to walk in a day

How far you walk in a day is obviously up to you and will depend on your fitness and experience. As a guide, people generally walk at about 2½ miles (4km) an hour. If you are planning to walk the whole length of the Thames Path, or for several days, it is usually sensible to plan a short first day to ease yourself in gently.

What to take with you

- Carry warm and waterproof clothing as even on some summer days wind and rain can make a walk or ride uncomfortable.

- Walkers should wear strong, comfortable footwear. During the summer trainers are usually OK for a walk on the Thames Path, but during wet periods and winter months don walking boots or even Wellingtons if you're comfortable walking in these. Take a blister repair kit, just in case.

- Wear protection (hat and lotion) against the sun during the summer.

- Carry water if walking for more than a couple of hours.

- If your walk is along unfamiliar paths don't forget your map and/or guidebook.

Weather information

• During winter months and occasionally at other times, some sections of the Path, especially in the upper reaches, can become flooded and unwalkable after heavy rain. To be sure of keeping your feet dry telephone the **Environment Agency's flood information line on 0845 988 1188 (1, 1, 1, 1) or visit www.environment-agency.gov.uk**

• Visit www.metoffice.gov.uk for general weather forecasts – the areas covering the Thames Path are South-East England & the West Country.

Personal safety

If you are walking alone it's sensible, as a simple precaution, to let someone know where you are and when you expect to arrive/return. Do bear in mind that mobile phone coverage can be patchy in rural areas, so you cannot always rely on it.

Dog matters

If you are planning to undertake a long distance walk along the Thames Path with your dog, you are advised to ensure it is fit before you start; on occasions walkers have had to abandon a walk because their dogs can't keep up!

Please also make sure your dog is under close control at all times to prevent it from disturbing livestock or wildlife. Whilst in fields with livestock you are asked to keep your dog on a lead, although on occasions cattle may harass you because of the dog and in such circumstances it is wise to let it off the lead.

Spring floods upstream of Castle Eaton

V HOW TO FOLLOW THE TRAIL

The Official National Trail Guides

National Trail Guides published by Aurum Press are available from the National Trails Office (see page 16).

Other Guides

Details of other guides and publications are on page 14.

Maps

It is a good idea to use maps when walking, particularly in unfamiliar areas. The official Guide includes colour sections of all the appropriate 1:25 000 Ordnance Survey maps needed to follow the Thames Path. Alternatively, for you to enjoy and interpret the wider landscape, you may wish to purchase your own OS maps.

The Landranger series (pink cover at 1:50 000 or 2cm to 1km) has all public rights of way, viewpoints, tourist information and selected places of interest marked on them.

The Explorer series (orange cover at 1:25 000 or 4cm to 1km) also includes fencelines which can be helpful, and more tourist information. For the whole of the Thames Path you will need:

Landranger		Explorer	
163	Cheltenham & Cirencester	168	Stroud, Tetbury & Malmesbury
164	Oxford	169	Cirencester and Swindon
174	Newbury and Wantage	170	Abingdon, Wantage and Vale of White Horse
175	Reading and Windsor		
176	West London	180	Oxford
177	East London	171	Chiltern Hills West
		172	Chiltern Hills East
		160	Windsor, Weybridge and Bracknell
		161	London South
		173	London North
		162	Greenwich and Gravesend

Signage

The Thames Path follows a series of well-signed public rights of way and a few roads which are mostly minor.

The acorn is the symbol of National Trails and is used on all Thames Path signage.

In most cases the signs, or waymark discs on gates or posts, will also carry the words 'Thames Path'. The status of the right of way, which defines who can use it, will also be shown either in words, or by using the national waymarking scheme of coloured arrows – see below:

Footpath

Bridleway

Restricted Byway

Byway

Hampton Court Palace

VI PUBLICATIONS

Publications about the Thames Path and River

There are many publications available about the River Thames and its Path of which the following is a selection:

National Trail Gudes (Official guides with written route descriptions and colour maps):

• **Thames Path - in the country** by David Sharp & Tony Gowers, Aurum Press 2012. Covers the Source of the Thames to Hampton Court.

• **Thames Path - in London** by Phoebe Clapham, Aurum Press 2012. Hampton Court to the Thames Barrier.

Thames Path Harvey Map 2012 – a waterproof map of the whole length of the Thames Path including information on facilities along the Trail.

The Thames Path: From the Sea to the Source by Leigh Hatts, Cicerone 2010 – a guide for those walking the Thames Path upstream.

Walks Along the Thames Path by Ron Emmons 2008 – 25 circular walks from Thames Head to Greenwich.

Hazel catkins

The following companies offer self-guided or guided holiday packages on part or all of the Thames Path:

Walking

Capital Sport – **T**: 01296 631671, www.capital-sport.co.uk

Contours Walking Holidays – **T**: 01629 821900, www.contours.co.uk

Footpath Holidays – **T**: 01985 840049, www.footpath-holidays.com

Let's Go Walking – **T**: 01837 880075, www.thamespathwalkingholidays.co.uk

Responsibletravel.com – **T**: 01273 600030, www.responsibletravel.com

Walk the Landscape – **T**: 07718 660070, www.walkthelandscape.co.uk

Explore Britain – **T**: 01740 650900, www.explorebritain.com

Please note, for those visiting the Thames Path independently, many of the accommodation providers listed in this guide are willing to collect you from and return you to the Trail. Many will also transport your luggage to your next night's accommodation.

Chiltern Hills from Gatehampton

VIII USEFUL CONTACTS

Thames Path Managers/National Trails Office

National Trails Managers, National Trails Office, Signal Court, Old Station Way, Eynsham OX29 4TL **T**: 01865 810224
E: Nationaltrails@oxfordshire.gov.uk

Highway Authorities responsible for public rights of way

Buckinghamshire County Council – **T**: 0845 370 8090 www.buckscc.gov.uk

Gloucestershire County Council – **T**: 01452 425000 www.gloucestershire.gov.uk

Oxfordshire County Council – **T**: 01865 810226 www.oxfordshire.gov.uk

Reading Borough Council – **T**: 0118 937 3737 www.reading.gov.uk

Royal Borough of Windsor and Maidenhead – **T**: 01628 683800 www.rbwm.gov.uk

Surrey County Council – **T**: 03456 009009 www.surreycc.gov.uk

Swindon Borough Council – **T**: 01793 445500 www.swindon.gov.uk

West Berkshire Council – **T**: 01635 42400 www.westberks.gov.uk

Wiltshire Council – **T**: 0300 456 0100 www.wiltshire.gov.uk

Wokingham Council – **T**: 0118 974 6000 www.wokingham.gov.uk

Agency responsible for National Trails

Natural England – **T**: 0845 600 3078 www.naturalengland.org.uk

Agency responsible for the River Thames

Environment Agency – **T**: 0870 850 6506 www.environment-agency.gov.uk

The Thames Path is exceptionally well served by public transport which makes it possible to explore the Trail without needing a car by using trains, buses or, unusually for a National Trail, boats. Please visit the map-based Travel Planner on the Thames Path website at www.nationaltrail.co.uk/thamespath to help you plan your journey.

• Rail Services	08457 484950 (24 hours a day)
	www.nationalrail.co.uk
• Bus Services	0871 200 2233
	www.traveline.info
• Boat Services	Visit the Thames Path Travel Planner at
	www.nationaltrail.co.uk/thamespath or
	the boating pages at www.visitthames.co.uk
• Public Transport in London	0843 222 1234
	www.tfl.gov.uk
• Taxi Services	Information is included at the start of each of the
	sections

We encourage people to use public transport rather than travelling by private car as this is better for the environment, helps to support local public transport services and reduces congestion from parking in the smaller settlements. However, those wishing to travel to the Thames Path by car are asked to park considerately if parking in villages on or close to the Trail. Other places to park are listed within each section.

X FOLLOW THE COUNTRY CODE

• Be safe – plan ahead and follow any signs

Even when going out locally, it's best to get the latest information about where and when you can go. Follow advice and local signs, and be prepared for the unexpected.

• Leave gates and property as you find them

Please respect the working life of the countryside, as our actions can affect people's livelihoods, our heritage, and the safety and welfare of animals and ourselves.

• Protect plants and animals, and take your litter home

We have a responsibility to protect our countryside now and for future generations, so make sure you don't harm animals, birds, plants or trees.

• Keep your dog under close control

The countryside is a great place to exercise dogs, but it's every owner's duty to make sure their dog is not a danger or nuisance to farm animals, wildlife or other people.

• Consider other people

Showing consideration and respect for other people makes the countryside a pleasant environment for everyone – at home, at work and at leisure.

For further details visit www.countrysideaccess.gov.uk

Near Donnington Bridge, Oxford

In emergency dial 999 and ask for the service required.

Police

Dial 101 for non-emergencies and you will be connected to the local police force.

Hospitals

The telephone numbers given are for the hospital switchboard; ask to be put through to Accident & Emergency Reception.

◆   Full 24-hour emergency service

▼   Minor injuries or first aid unit, some not a 24-hour service

Section	Town/City	Telephone No	Address
1	◆ ▼ Cirencester	01285 655711	Cirencester Hospital, The Querns, Tetbury Road, Cirencester GL7 1UY
1,2 & 3	◆ Swindon	01793 604020	The Great Western Hospital, Marlborough Road, Swindon SN3 6BB
3,4 & 5	◆ Oxford	01865 741166	John Radcliffe Hospital, Headley Way, Headington, Oxford OX3 9DU
5 & 6	▼ Abingdon	01235 205730	Abingdon Community Hospital, Marcham Road, OX14 1AG
6 & 7	▼ Wallingford	01491 208500	Wallingford Community Hospital, Reading Road, Wallingford OX10 9DU
7 & 8	◆ Reading	0118 322 5111	The Royal Berkshire Hospital, London Road, Reading RG1 5AN
8 & 9	▼ Henley	01491 637400	Townlands Hospital, York Rd, Henley-on-Thames RG9 2EB
9 & 10	◆ ▼ High Wycombe	01494 526161	Wycombe General Hospital, Queen Alexandra Road, High Wycombe HP11 2TT
10 & 11	◆ Slough	01753 633000	Wexham Park Hospital, Wexham Street, Slough SL2 4HL

XI EMERGENCY CONTACTS

Hospitals cont.

Section	Town/City	Telephone No	Address
11 & 12	◆ Chertsey	01932 872000	St Peter's Hospital, Guildford Road, Chertsey KT16 0PZ
12	◆ Kingston-upon-Thames	020 8546 7711	Kingston Hospital, Galsworthy Road, Kingston-upon-Thames KT2 7QB
13	◆ Isleworth	020 8560 2121	West Middlesex University Hospital, Twickenham Road, Isleworth TW7 6AF
13 & 14	◆ Hammersmith	020 8846 1234	Charing Cross Hospital, Fulham Palace Road, London W6 8RF
14	◆ Chelsea	020 8746 8000	Chelsea & Westminster Hospital, 369 Fulham Road, London SW10 9NH
14	◆ Lambeth	020 7188 7188	St Thomas's Hospital, Westminster Bridge Road, London SE1 7EH
14 & 15	▼ The City	020 7188 7188	Guy's Hospital, Great Maze Pond, London SE1 9RT
15	◆ Dartford	01322 428100	Darent Valley Hospital, Darent Wood Road, Dartford DA2 8DA

Trout at Tadpole Bridge

Accommodation, Facilities & Services

The following chapters give details of the settlements, accommodation, eating places, shops, attractions and other facilities along the Thames Path. They are listed in geographic order from the source of the river to the Thames Barrier in London.

If you fail to find accommodation using this guide please contact the Visitor Information Centres listed near the beginning of each section which may be able to provide other addresses. Some towns and cities, including London, have such an extensive range and number of places to stay that details of individual establishments are not listed in this guide.

To find map grid references for individual accommodation put postcodes into www.nearby.org.uk

You are strongly advised to book accommodation in advance. Whilst booking, do check prices since those quoted here are usually the minimum charged. It's also wise to book evening meals in advance if eating in village pubs as they can get very busy.

For those who would like to enjoy more than a day on the Thames Path without having to carry all their possessions, quite a few accommodation providers have indicated whether they are willing to transport the luggage you don't need during the day to your next night's accommodation. The fee charged for this service needs to be discussed and agreed at the time of the booking. Accommodation providers have also indicated if they are willing to collect you from the Thames Path and deliver you back after your stay.

All the information within this Companion is as accurate as possible. Inclusion of accommodation does not constitute a recommendation although it is indicated in the details whether an establishment has a recognised grade awarded to it. If you have any comments or notice any errors, please write to the National Trails Manager responsible for this guide (page 16).

XII ACCOMMODATION, FACILITIES AND SERVICES

Key to Symbols for Settlements

Any comments relate to preceding icon.

map grid reference (see start of each section for relevant maps)

shortest walking distance from the Thames Path

most convenient train station

P£ car park (paying)

P F car park (free)

toilets

&WC toilets adapted for disabled users

Visitor Information Centre

pub (usually open lunchtimes 11am-3pm then evenings 6pm-11pm). Names and telephone numbers of pubs are given for those settlements with up to two pubs

✕ bar meals in pub

✉ post office (usual opening hours 9am-5.30pm weekdays; 9am-12.30pm Sat)

general store (usual opening hours 9am-5.30pm Mon-Sat)

cafe/tea shop

restaurant

food take-away

S M T W T F S opening hours of services relate to the preceding symbol

eg: open all day ▮▮ closed all day

Post offices, general stores, cafe/tea shops – open morning; Pubs, bar meals, restaurants, takeaways – open lunchtime

Post offices, general stores, cafe/tea shops – open afternoon; Pubs, bar meals, restaurants, takeaways – open evening

£ bank (usually open daily 9.30am-4.30pm Mon-Fri)

cash machine available, including outside bank opening hours

☆ tourist attraction

Key to Symbols for Accommodation

Type of accommodation (symbols in margins)

▲ hostel   🏠 inn

🛆 camping   B&B bed and breakfast

🏠 hotel   SC self catering

The number and price following the symbols for rooms gives the number and price of that type of room available. The same applies to tent/caravan pitches. Prices quoted for rooms are the minimum price per room per night for bed and breakfast. The price for single occupancy of double or twin rooms is given in brackets eg (£45).

Accommodation symbols – hotels, inns, guest houses, B&Bs and hostels

🛏	double room	🎒	packed lunches available
🛏	twin room	🍴	evening meals available at accommodation or locally
🛏	family room		
🛏	single room	**DRY**	clothes/boots drying facilities
⊖	smoking bedroom(s) available	▣	laundry facilities
✦✦	children welcome	🚗	transport to and from Trail by arrangement
♿	wheelchair access		
🐕	dogs allowed by arrangement	🎒	luggage transported to next overnight stop by arrangement
V	caters for vegetarians	📶	free Wifi
◗	most food locally produced	VISA	credit card(s) and/or Paypal accepted
◗	some food locally produced		
●	most food is organic	★	VisitEngland accommodation standard
O	some food is organic		
		⋈	special feature/comment

23

XII ACCOMMODATION, FACILITIES AND SERVICES

Accommodation symbols – camping and caravan sites

⛺	tent pitches	🚿	showers
🚐	caravan pitches	⬛	laundry facilities
🚰	cold water	🎲	site shop
🚰	hot water	CG	camping gas available
🚻	toilets	⊦	special feature/comment
♿WC	toilets adapted for disabled users		

Close to the source of the Thames

Section 1

The Source to Cricklade

This rural first 12 miles (20km) of the Thames Path is within the fine countryside of the Cotswolds where farming and small stone-built settlements dominate. The river grows from nothing to a narrow waterway by the time it reaches Cricklade.

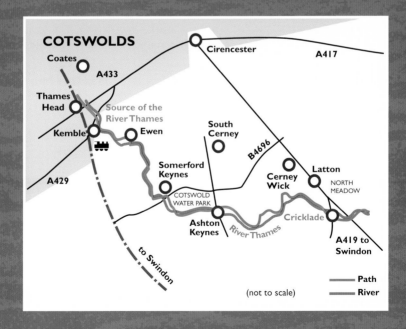

Maps

Landranger maps	163	Cheltenham & Cirencester
Explorer maps	168	Stroud, Tetbury & Malmesbury
	169	Cirencester & Swindon

Taxi Services

Place	Name	Telephone numbers
Cirencester	Aristocabs	01285 640926
	A2B Taxis	01285 655651
	Centurion Taxis	01285 659288
	Cirencester Radio Cars	01285 650850
	Cirencester Taxis	01285 800131
	Home James	01285 641339
	Kemble Station Taxi	01285 642767
Siddington	P & A Travel	07946 006847/01285 657983

Car Parking

The following is a list of public car parks close to the Thames Path and does not include on-street parking in villages or towns. Where there are several car parks in a town, those closest to the Path have been listed. Unfortunately theft from vehicles parked in the countryside does occasionally occur, so please leave valuables you don't want to carry at home.

Place	Map Grid Reference
Neigh Bridge Country Park, off Spine Road West 1/2 mile south of Somerford Keynes	SU 018947
Waterhay Bridge, 1 mile southeast of Ashton Keynes	SU 060933
Cricklade Town Hall	SU 100935

Toilets

Place	Map Grid Reference
Cricklade, off High Street ♿	SU 100937

Visitor Information Centres

*Offers accommodation booking service for personal callers during opening hours

Place	Address/Opening Hours
*Cirencester	The Corinium Museum, Park Street, Cirencester GL7 2BX **T**: 01285 654180 www.cotswold.gov.uk **Opening hours** Summer (Apr-Oct): Mon-Sat 10:00-17:00; Sun 14:00-17:00 Winter (Nov-Mar): Mon-Sat 10:00-16:00; Sun 14:00-16:00 (closed 23-26 Dec & 1 Jan)
*Swindon	Central Library, Regent Circus, Swindon SN1 1QG **T**: 01793 466454 **E:** infocentre@swindon.gov.uk www.visitwiltshire.co.uk/swindon **Opening hours** All year: Mon-Sat 10:00-16:00
Cricklade	Town Council Office, 113 High Street, Cricklade SN6 6AE **T**: 01793 751394 www.cricklade-tc.gov.uk **Opening hours** All year: Mon-Thur 10:00-17:00; Fri 10:00-16:30; Sat 10:00-13:00

CIRENCESTER

 **SP0201** 3miles (5km)
Kemble 5miles (8km)

Town with full range of services, visit www.cirencester.gov.uk for further details. It has a wide range of accommodation – details from Visitor Information Centre (see section introduction).

☆ Corinium Museum **T**: 01285 655611
www.coriniummuseum.cotswold.co.uk

☆ New Brewery Arts Centre **T**: 01285 657181 www.newbreweryarts.org.uk

☆ Roman Ampitheatre www.cotswolds.org/roman-amphitheatre-cirencester
Open all the time and free entrance

COATES

 **SO9801** 1.3miles (2km)
Kemble 3.4miles (5.5km)

Pub: Tunnel House Inn 01285 770280

Tunnel House Inn

Michael Hughes
Tarlton Road, Coates, Cirencester GL7 6PW
T: 01285 770280
E: info@tunnelhouse.com
www.tunnelhouse.com
40 £9 WC
Most major cards
Pub on site serving meals.

27

THAMES HEAD

ST9899 400m
Kemble 1.2miles (2km)

S M T W T F S   S M T W T F S

Pub: Thames Head Inn 01285 770259

Thames Head   closed 25 & 26 Dec

Nicola and Ben King
Tetbury Road, Cirencester GL7 6NZ
T: 01285 770259
E: info@thamesheadinn.co.uk
www.thamesheadinn.co.uk

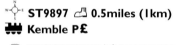

3 £75   1 £90 (£50)   1 £50

All major cards. All rooms en-suite

KEMBLE

ST9897 0.5miles (1km)
Kemble P£

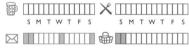

S M T W T F S   S M T W T F S

S M T W T F S   S M T W T F S

£ Inside village shop
Pub: Tavern 01285 770216

☆ Thames Severn Canal
www.cotswoldcanals.com

The Stables   SC

Ms Rowena Paul
Forge House, Limes Road, Kemble GL7 6FS
T: 01285 771157
info@forgehousekemble.co.uk
www.forgehousekemble.co.uk
Self-catering 2 bed cottage (sleeps 4) All rooms en-suite £574/week ★★★★★

Willows   B&B

Mrs K Wilkinson
2 Glebe Lane, Kemble GL7 6BD
T: 01285 770667 **M:** 07759 920490
www.willowskemble.co.uk

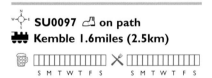

1 £60   1 £70   1 £55

(min age 12) Twin room en-suite

Double room has private bathroom

EWEN

SU0097 on path
Kemble 1.6miles (2.5km)

S M T W T F S   S M T W T F S

Pub: Wild Duck Inn 01285 770310
☆ Cirencester Park
T: 01285 640410
www.cirencesterpark.co.uk

B&B Well Cottage

Mr Neil Pass
Ewen, Cirencester GL7 6BU
T: 01285 770212 **M:** 07850 328447
E: neil@wellcottagebandb.co.uk
www.wellcottagebandb.co.uk
🛏 2 £65 ⛌ 1 £65 (£50) ♿ V ❦
O 🐕 🛜 💳 All major cards & Paypal
★★★★ All rooms en-suite
🅷 VisitEngland Silver Award

B&B Brooklands Farm

Mrs E M Crew
Ewen, Cirencester GL7 6BU
T: 01285 770487
E: ScarlettCREW1@gmail.com
🛏 1 £60 ⛌ 1 £60 V ● 🅳🆁🆈 ⬛ 🚗
🐕 ★★
One room en-suite.

INN Wild Duck

Mrs Tina Mussell
Ewen, Cirencester GL7 6BY
T: 01285 770310
E: tinamussell@aol.com
www.thewildduckinn.co.uk
🛏 12 £110 (£70) 👪 ♿ 🖼 V 🔥 🚫
● 🍎 O 🅳🆁🆈 🚗 🐕 🛜 💳 Most major
cards ★★★★ All rooms en-suite

SOMERFORD KEYNES

◈ **SU0195** ⬒ **0.3miles (0.5km)**
🚂 **Kemble 3.7miles (6km)**

🍺 |||||||||||||| ✕ ||||||||||||||
   S M T W T F S   S M T W T F S

Pub: Baker's Arms 01285 861298.

☆ Cotswold Water Park
T: 01793 752413
www.waterpark.org

Orchard Cottage *Closed Jan and May-Aug* **SC**

Stephen Perkin
No 3 Mill Village, Lower Mill Estate,
Cirencester GL7 6FP
T: 01494 729234 **M:** 07766 532319
E: steve@cotswoldcottages-onthames.co.uk
www.cotswoldcottages-onthames.co.uk
🅷 Self-catering from £85/night.

Flowering Clematis

29

SOUTH CERNEY

 **SU0597** 2miles (3.2km)
Kemble 4.4miles (7km)

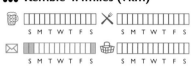

S M T W T F S   S M T W T F S

S M T W T F S   S M T W T F S

In village shop

☆ Cotswold Water Park
T: 01793 752413
www.waterpark.org

SC **Lower Mill Holidays** *6th Jan-6th Feb*

Mr Mark Thomas
The Gateway Centre, Lake 6, Spine
Road East, South Cerney, Cirencester
GL7 5TL
T: 01285 861839
E: contact@orionholidays.com
www.orionholidays.com
Self-catering accommodation from
£512/Friday to Monday.

B&B **Mallin**

Mr Malcom Hood
49 Meadow Way, South Cerney,
Cirencester GL7 6HY
T: 01285 869080 **M:** 07817 630927
E: linda@lcs-mcm.co.uk
www.mallinbandb.co.uk
1£50 1 £50 (£35) V O 🛜 ★★

Tanners **B&B**

Mrs Julia Delamain
High Street, South Cerney, Cirencester
GL7 5UP
T: 01285 861283 **M:** 07775 520955
E: juliadelamain@yahoo.co.uk
www.southcerneybedandbreakfast.co.uk

2 £65 1 £65 ★★ 🔲 V 🔥 🌑
🍎 DRY
Packed lunches and evening meals by
prior arrangement.

ASHTON KEYNES

SU0494 on path
Kemble 5.7miles (9.2km) PF

S M T W T F S   S M T W T F S

S M T W T F S   S M T W T F S

Pub: White Hart Inn 01285 861247

☆ Cotswold Water Park
T: 01793 752413
www.waterpark.org

Wheatleys Farm **B&B**

Mrs Gill Freeth
High Road, Ashton Keynes, Swindon
SN6 6NX
T: 01285 861310
E: gill@wheatleysfarm.co.uk
www.wheatleysfarm.co.uk
1 £70 1 (£100) ★★ (min age
12) V 🔥 🍸 O DRY 🔲 🐾 🛜 ★★★★
All rooms en-suite
VisitEngland Silver Award

B&B Cove House *Closed Xmas & New Year*

Mrs Valerie Threlfall
1 Cove House, Cove House Gardens,
Ashton Keynes, Swindon SN6 6NS
T: 01285 861226
E: roger@covehouse.co.uk
www.covehouse.co.uk
🛏 2 £80 🛏 1 £75 (£55) ⚥ V ❖
O DRY ▣ 👪 📶 All rooms en-suite

🍴 Transport provided to other pubs
when local pub not serving food

B&B The Firs

Ms Karen Shaw
High Road, Ashton Keynes, Swindon
SN6 6NX
T: 01285 860458 **M:** 07989 857435
E: thefirsbb@yahoo.co.uk
🛏 2 £50 🛏 1 £50 (£40) 🛏 2 £35
⚥ ❖ V 🌾 ◐ ❖ O DRY ▣ 👪 📶
Some rooms en-suite
🍴 Evening meals only at weekends

B&B The Longhouse

Mrs Liz Chick
17 High Road, Ashton Keynes, Swindon
SN6 6NL
T: 01285 861317
E: lizzie_chick@yahoo.com
🛏 1 £60 (£35) 🛏 1 £70 🛏 1 £30 ⚥
🌾 ❖ O DRY 📶 Some rooms en-suite

CERNEY WICK

◈ **SU0796** 👢 1mile (1.6km)
🚂 Kemble 6.9miles (11.1km)

S M T W T F S   S M T W T F S

Pub: Crown Inn 01793 750369

Long House **B&B**

Nic and Nicola Wade
Cerney Wick, Cirencester GL7 5QH
T: 01285 719444 **M:** 07764 760840
E: enquiries@
thelonghousebedandbreakfast.co.uk
www.thelonghousebedandbreakfast.
co.uk
🛏 2 £60 🛏 1£60 🛏 1 £30 ⚥ ❖
V 🌾 ❖ O DRY ▣ 🚗 👪 🚗 📶 VISA
Paypal

LATTON

◈ **SU0995** 👢 1.6miles (2.5km)
🚂 Swindon 9.3miles (15km)

Dolls House **B&B**

Mrs Gemma Maraffi
The Street, Latton, Cricklade SN6 6DJ
T: 01793 750384 **M:** 07762 619049
E: gemma-maraffi@bbdollshouse.freeserve.
co.uk
🛏 1 £60 🛏 1 £40 ⚥ (min age 12)
♿ ❖ V 🌾 ◐ 🍎 ● DRY 🚗 👪 📶
★★★ All rooms en-suite
🍴 Evening meals weedays only. Lift
provided to local pub

CRICKLADE

⊕ SU0993 ⌂ on path
🚂 Swindon 7.8miles (12.5km)

Small town with full range of services, visit
www.cricklade-tc.gov.uk for more details

☆ Cricklade Museum
T: 01793 750686
www.cricklademuseum.org

☆ North Meadow National Nature
Reserve   www.naturalengland.org.uk

☆ Swindon & Cricklade Railway
T: 01793 771615 (weekends only)
www.swindon-cricklade-railway.org

Red Lion

Mr Tom Gee
74 High Street, Cricklade SN6 6DD
T: 01793 750776
E: info@theredlioncricklade.co.uk
www.theredlioncricklade.co.uk
🛏/🛏 5 £80 👫👶🖐 🎒 V 🍺🍏🍽🔴
📶 💳 Most major cards ★★★★ All
rooms en-suite
🏠 No evening meals served on Sundays.
Pull-out bed available for £20

Cricklade House

Mr Paul Butler
Common Hill, Cricklade SN6 6HA
T: 01793 750751
E: reception@crickladehotel.co.uk
www.crickladehotel.co.uk
🛏 41 £80 🛏 3 £80 (£60) 🛏 2
£80 + £25/child 🛏 2 £60 👫👶🖐 🎒 V
🍺🍏🍴🔳📶💳 Most major cards.
★★★ All rooms en-suite
🏠 Hotel is 1km west of Cricklade

Upper Chelworth Farm   B&B

Mrs Helen Hopkins
Cricklade SN6 6HD
T: 01793 750440
🛏 2 £50 🛏 1 £52 (£35) 🛏 1 £60
🛏 2 £30 👫👶 (min age 5) 🎒 V 🍴 🚗 📶
★★★ All rooms en-suite
🏠 Farm is 2km west of Cricklade

Vale Hotel

Mrs Maria Franca-Landure
32 High Street, Cricklade SN6 6AY
T: 01793 750223 M: 07927 175296
E: enquiries@valehotel.net
www.valehotel.net
🛏 7 £55 🛏 5 £39 👫👶 V 🍺🍏🍴🔵🔳
📶 💳 Most major cards ★★★ All rooms
en-suite

B&B SC

Latton Alpacas

Mrs Mym Holcombe
Autumn Lodge Farm, Malmesbury Road,
Leigh, Cricklade SN6 6RA
T: 01793 751195 **M:** 07721 586071
E: mym@lattonalpacas.co.uk
www.lattonalpacas.co.uk

🛏 1 £50 V 🐾 ⓘ ◑ DRY 🚗 🚶 📶
💳 Most major cards

🍴 B&B is 2km west of Cricklade.
Camping in a yurt, March to Oct, min
stay 3 nights, £50/night. Craft courses,
alpaca experience and craft shop also
available

White Hart Hotel 🏨

Mr John Flynn
High Street, Cricklade SN6 6AA
T: 01793 750206
E: info@thewhitehartcricklade.co.uk
www.thewhitehartcricklade.co.uk

🛏 6 £63 🛏 3 £63 🛏 2 £80
🛏 2 £50 👫 📷 V 🐾 ◑ ⓘ DRY 🚶 📶 💳

Most major cards. All rooms en-suite
🍴 Continental breakfast only. No evening
meal on Sundays

Cricklade High Street

Section 2

Cricklade to Lechlade

This 11 miles (18km) of quiet countryside between the
two small rural towns sees the River Thames grow to a
respectable body of water with boats regularly using the
final short stretch before Lechlade.

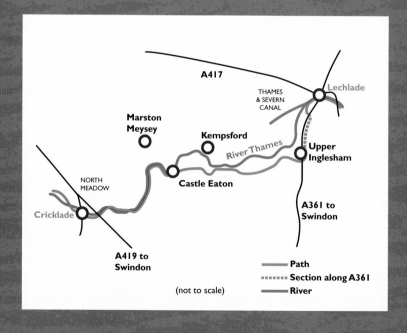

A417

THAMES
& SEVERN
CANAL

Lechlade

Marston
Meysey

Kempsford

River Thames

Upper
Inglesham

Castle Eaton

NORTH
MEADOW

Cricklade

A361 to
Swindon

A419 to
Swindon

Path

Section along A361

(not to scale)

River

Please Note

This part of the Thames Path includes a temporary section along the main A361 road whilst a final route for the National Trail nearer the river is created and it is best negotiated by taxi or bus. Taxi details are below and there are regular bus services except on Sundays - check traveline on www.traveline.info or call them on 0871 200 2233.

Maps

Landranger maps	163	Cheltenham & Cirencester
Explorer maps	169	Cirencester & Swindon
	170	Abingdon, Wantage & Vale of White Horse

Taxi Services

Place	Name	Telephone numbers
Lechlade	CATs Cars	01367 253424/07824 649201
	CTs	01367 252575

Car Parking

The following is a list of public car parks close to the Thames Path and does not include on-street parking in villages or towns. Where there are several car parks in a town, those closest to the Path have been listed. Unfortunately theft from vehicles parked in the countryside does occasionally occur, so please leave valuables you don't want to carry at home.

Place	Map Grid Reference
Cricklade Town Hall	SU 100935
Lechlade Riverside, on A361 1/2 mile south of Lechlade	SU 211990

Toilets

Place	Map Grid Reference
Cricklade, off High Street ♿	SU 100937
Lechlade, Burford Street ♿	SU 214997
Lechlade, St John's Lock	SU 222990

Visitor Information Centres

*Offers accommodation booking service for personal callers during opening hours

Place	Address/Opening Hours
Cricklade	Town Council Office, 113 High Street, Cricklade SN6 6AE **T**: 01793 751394 www.cricklade-tc.gov.uk
	Opening hours All year: Mon-Thur 10:00-17:00; Fri 10:00-16:30; Sat 10:00-13:00
*Swindon	Central Library, Regent Circus, Swindon SN1 1QG **T**: 01793 466454 **E**: infocentre@swindon.gov.uk www.visitwiltshire.co.uk/swindon
	Opening hours All year: Mon-Sat 10:00-16:00
*Faringdon	The Corn Exchange, Gloucester Street, Faringdon SN7 7JA **T**: 01367 242191 www.faringdon.org/tttourism1.htm
	Opening hours: All year: Mon-Fri 9:00-14:00; Sat 9:30-13:00

CASTLE EATON

SU1495 🛏 on path
🚂 Swindon 8.6miles (13.8km)

S M T W T F S   S M T W T F S

Pubs: Red Lion 01285 810280

Red Lion

Mrs Melody-Ann Lyall
The Street, Castle Eaton SN6 6JZ
T: 01285 810280
E: m.lyall@btconnect.com
www.red-lion.co.uk
🛏 2 £60 🛏 1 £60 (£45) 🛏 1
£120 ♥♥ V 🐾 ◐ 🍎 O DRY 🚗 ♿
🛜 VISA Most major cards. ★★★ Some
rooms en-suite

Malt House   B&B

Mrs Tayma Wallbridge
The Street, Castle Eaton SN6 6JZ
T: 01285 810822
E: tayma.wallbridge@gmail.com
🛏 1 £70 V 🐾 ◐ O DRY ♿ 🛜 All
rooms en-suite

Wild rose

Marston Meysey

SU1297  **2.4miles (3.8km)**
🚂 **Swindon 10.6miles (17km)**

🍺 ▯▯▯▯▯▯▯▯▯▯▯ ✕ ▯▯▯▯▯▯▯▯▯▯
S M T W T F S   S M T W T F S

Pub: The Old Spotted Cow 01285
810264

Second Chance Touring Park
Closed Dec-Feb

Mrs B Stroud
Second Chance, Marston Meysey SN6 6SZ
T: 01285 810675
⛺ 22 £6 🚐 26 £12 🚰 ♨ Ⓦ🅿️🔲
🍴 Prices are per person/night

Kempsford

SU1696  **1.1miles (1.8km)**
🚂 **Swindon 11.2miles (18km) PF**

🍺 ▯▯▯▯▯▯▯▯▯▯▯ ✕ ▯▯▯▯▯▯▯▯▯▯
S M T W T F S   S M T W T F S

Pub: George 01285 810236

B&B Kempsford Manor

Mrs Z I Williamson
High Street, Kempsford, Fairford
GL7 4EQ
T: 01285 810131 **M:** 07980 543882
E: info@kempsfordmanor.com
www.kempsfordmanor.com
🛏 2 £70 🛏 1 £75 (£45) 🛏 2 £45
♀♂ 📺 V ♨️🅾️ 🕯️🅾️ DRY 🔲 🚗 📶
★★★ Some rooms en-suite
🍴 Evening meal by prior arrangement

Upper Inglesham

SU2096  **on path**
🚂 **Swindon 9 miles (14.5km)**

🎫 ▮▮▮▮▮▮▮▮▮▮
S M T W T F S

Restaurant: Inglesham Forge 01367 252298

Evergreen B&B

Mr & Mrs Blowen
3 College Farm Cottages, Upper
Inglesham, Swindon SN6 7QU
T: 01367 253407
E: ingridgreen1947@hotmail.com
www.evergreen-cotswold.co.uk
🛏 1 £55 🛏 2 £33 ♀♂ (min age 14)
♨️ DRY 📶

St Mary's Church, Kempsford

LECHLADE

☆ **SU2199** 👣 **on path**
🚂 **Swindon 10.9miles (17.5km)**
Small town with full range of services, for further details visit
www.lechladeonthames.co.uk

☆ Lechlade and Bushyleaze Trout Fisheries
T: 01367 253266
www.lechladetrout.co.uk

B&B Cambrai Lodge

Mr John Titchener
Oak Street, Lechlade GL7 3AY
T: 01367 253173 **M:** 07860 150467
E: cambrailodge@btconnect.com
www.cambrailodgeguesthouse.co.uk
🛏 3 £65 🛏 3 £65 (£50) ♛♜ 🕮 V
🅰 DRY 🐾 🛜 💳 Paypal ★★★★ All rooms en-suite
🅷 Can leave car while walking trail, fee by arrangement

Riverside 🏨

Roger Waite
Park End Wharf, Lechlade GL7 3AQ
T: 01367 252534
E: riverside@arkells.com
www. theriverside-lechlade.com
🛏 3 £84 🛏 3 £84 (£54) 🛏
2 £114 🛏 3 £54 ♛♜ (min age 5) **V**
🌑 🕮 O 🐾 🛜 💳 All major cards
★★★All rooms en-suite
🅷 No evening meals on Sundays

Denbigh B&B

Mr John Shearer
Spring Gardens, Lechlade GL7 3AY
T: 01367 252806
🛏 1 £60 (£35) 🛏 1 £30 ♛♜ (min age 5) ♿ 🕮 V 🅰 🍎 ● ● DRY 🅾 🐾 🛜

Bridge House Camp Site ⛺
Closed Nov-end March or Easter if earlier

Mrs Karen Milsom-Shail
Bridge House, Thames St, Lechlade GL7 3AG
T: 01367 252348 **M:** 07733 015491
E: shailkevin@aol.com
⛺ 30 £8 🚐 37 £8 🕮 ⛽ 🚿 🚻
♿WC 🖩 🅾
🅷 Prices are per person/night

The Roundhouse,
upstream of Lechlade

Section 3

Lechlade to Newbridge

This 16miles (26km) is the longest section of the Thames Path following the ever-growing river as it slowly winds its way through the flat flood plain of the Thames Valley. It is wonderfully remote and therefore a good section to explore for those wanting peace and quiet, large skies and long views.

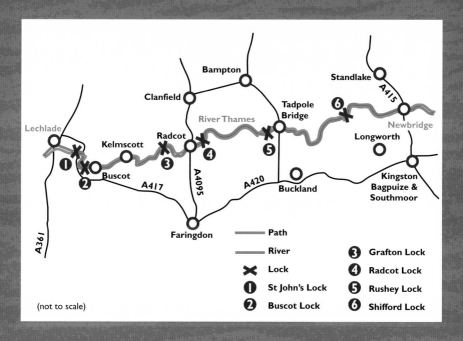

(not to scale)

Path

River

Lock

❶ St John's Lock

❷ Buscot Lock

❸ Grafton Lock

❹ Radcot Lock

❺ Rushey Lock

❻ Shifford Lock

Maps

Landranger maps	163	Cheltenham & Cirencester
	164	Oxford
Explorer maps	170	Abingdon, Wantage & Vale of White Horse
	180	Oxford

Taxi Services

Place	Name	Telephone numbers
Lechlade	CATs Cars	01367 253424/07824 649201
	CTs	01367 252575
Carterton	Charlie's Taxis	01993 845253
	Mark One Taxis	01993 840405
	MJ Taxis	01993 800999
Faringdon	Webb Cars	01367 241820
Bampton	Bampton Cars	01993 851900
Southmoor	Southmoor Taxis	01865 820984

Car Parking

The following is a list of public car parks close to the Thames Path and does not include on-street parking in villages or towns. Where there are several car parks in a town/city, those closest to the Path have been listed. Unfortunately theft from vehicles parked in the countryside does occasionally occur, so please leave valuables you don't want to carry at home.

Place	Map Grid Reference
Lechlade Riverside, on A361 ½ mile south of Lechlade	SU 211990
Buscot	SU 231977
Radcot Bridge (Only for patrons of Swan Hotel)	SU 285995

Toilets 🚻 & ♿ and Water Points at Locks 🚰

Place	Map Grid Reference
Lechlade, Burford Street 🚻 ♿	SU 214997
Lechlade, St John's Lock 🚻 🚰	SU 222990
Buscot 🚻 ♿	SU 231976
Grafton Lock 🚻	SU 272993
Radcot Lock 🚻 🚰	SP 292002
Rushey Lock 🚻 ♿ 🚰	SP 323001
Shifford Lock 🚻	SP 371010

Visitor Information Centres

*Offers accommodation booking service for personal callers during opening hours.

Place	Address/Opening Hours
*Faringdon	The Corn Exchange, Gloucester Street, Faringdon SN7 7JA **T**: 01367 242191 www.faringdon.org/tttourism1.htm **Opening hours:** All year: Mon-Fri 9:00-14:00; Sat 9:30-13:00
*Witney	3 Welch Way, Witney OX28 6JH **T**: 01993 775802 **E**: witney.vic@westoxon.gov.uk www.oxfordhsirecotswolds.org **Opening hours:** All year: Mon-Fri 9:00-17:00; Sat 9:30-17:00

BUSCOT

SU2397 0.4miles (0.6km)

Swindon 11.2miles (18km) PF

&WC

H Teashop winter opening: Fri, Sat, Sun
10:00-16:00

☆ Buscot Park
T: 01367 240932
www.buscot-park.com

☆ Buscot Village National Trust Property
T: 01793 762209
www.nationaltrust.org.uk

Buscot Manor B&B

Ms Romney Pargeter
Buscot, Lechlade SN7 8DA
T: 01367 252225 **M:** 07973 831690
E: romneypargeter@hotmail.co.uk
www.buscotmanor.co.uk

2 £85 1 £85 (£65) 1 £85

1 £65 V O DRY

 ★★★★★

H Activity breaks available.

KELMSCOTT

SU2599 0.3miles (0.5km)

Swindon 14miles (22.5km)

Pub: Plough Inn 01367 253543

☆ Kelmscott Manor
T: 01367 252486
www.kelmscottmanor.co.uk

B&B **Manor Farm** *Closed Xmas & New Year*

Mrs Emma Horner
Kelmscott, Lechlade GL7 3HJ
T: 01367 252620
E: emma@kelmscottbandb.co.uk
www.kelmscottbandb.co.uk
🛏 2 £65 🛏 1 £65 (£45) ♟ V🔥🍎
O DRY 🛜 All rooms en-suite.

Photo: Richard Kevern

Manor Farm

Tel: 01367 252620
www.kelmscottbandb.co.uk

17th century National Trust
farmhouse with a friendly,
relaxed atmosphere. Situated
on a working family farm
in the quiet, rural village of
Kelmscott, 5 minutes walk from
the Thames Path. Aga cooked
farmhouse breakfasts made with
local produce. Large rooms and
guest lounge with TV.

Plough Inn INN

Miss Josie Arnold
Kelmscott, Lechlade GL7 3HG
T: 01367 253543
E: josie.plough@hotmail.co.uk
🛏 5 £100 🛏 2 £85 🛏 1 £65 ♟
🔲 V🔥🌀🍎 O DRY 🐾🛜 💳 Most
major cards. All rooms en-suite

RADCOT

🧭 **SU2899** 🥾 **on path**
🚂 www.kelmscottbandb.co.uk

S M T W T F S   S M T W T F S

Pub: Swan 01367 810220

Swan *Closed Nov-March* ⛺

Mr Stephen Cocker
Radcot, Bampton OX18 2SX
T: 01367 810220
E: swanhotel@swanhotelradcot.co.uk
www.swanhotelradcot.co.uk
⛺ 35 £8 🚐 20 £15 🔲 🚿 🚰 ♿
CG 💳 Most major cards.
🍴 Meals and adapted WCs at the pub.

FARINGDON

 **SU2895** 🥾 **2.8miles (4.5km)**
🚂 **Swindon 12.2miles (19.5km)**

Town with full range of services, visit www.faringdon.org for further details. It has a wide range of accommodation – details from Visitor Information Centre (see section introduction).

☆ Faringdon Folly
T: 0845 475 8386
www.faringdonfolly.org.uk

CLANFIELD

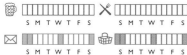 **SP2801** 🥾 **1.8miles (2.9km)**
🚂 **Shipton, but Oxford offers best rail & bus connect 9.9miles (16km) PF**

Pubs: Clanfield Tavern 01367 810223 & Cotswold Plough Hotel 01367 810222.

Ⓗ **Cotswold Plough Hotel** *closed Xmas*

Mr Martin Agius
Bourton Road, Clanfield OX18 2RB
T: 01367 810222
E: bookings@theploughclanfield.co.uk
www.cotswoldploughhotel.com
🛏 11 £110 🛏 2 £110 (£75) 👫 ♿
🐕 V 🖌 🌙 🍴 🅾 DRY 👣 🛜 💳 Most major cards ★★★ All rooms en-suite.

BAMPTON

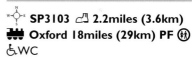 **SP3103** 🥾 **2.2miles (3.6km)**
🚂 **Oxford 18miles (29km) PF** 👤
♿WC

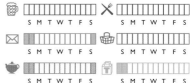

£ HSBC 🏧

For further information on Bampton visit www.bamptonoxon.co.uk

Coach House *closed Xmas New Year* B&B

Mr Robin Shuckburgh
Clanfield Road, Weald, Bampton OX18 2HG
T: 01993 851041 **M:** 07910 671892
E: info@thecoachhousebampton.co.uk
www.thecoachhousebampton.co.uk
🛏 3 £85 🛏 1 £115 (10% discount)
🛏 1 £130 👫 (min age 10) 🐕 V
🍎 🅾 DRY 🚗 👣 🛜 ★★★★ All rooms en-suite.
🅷 VisitEngland Gold and Breakfast Awards. Lift provided to local pubs/restaurants.

Blackthorn

Wheelgate House

Tel: 01993 851151
www.wheelgatehouse.co.uk

4★ Bed & Breakfast and home to 'Biztro', our warm and friendly restaurant, offering freshly cooked, locally produced, seasonal food served in the comfortable, cosy charm of our Cotswold stone house. Biztro open Tues-Sat for lunch and evening meals.

B&B | **Wheelgate House**

Ms Elizabeth Gooddy
Market Square, Bampton OX18 2JH
T: 01993 851151 **M:** 07747 466151
E: enquiries@wheelgatehouse.co.uk
www.wheelgatehouse.co.uk
2 £85 1 £85 (£55)
Most major cards ★★★★ All rooms en-suite.
No evening meals on Sundays & Mondays.

TADPOLE BRIDGE

 **SP3300** on path
Oxford 15.5miles (25km)

S M T W T F S   S M T W T F S

Pub: Trout Inn 01367 870382 – closed Sunday evenings during winter

Trout at Tadpole Bridge *Closed 25&26 Dec*

Mrs Helen Pugh
Tadpole Bridge, Buckland Marsh,
Faringdon SN7 8RF
T: 01367 870382
E: info@trout-inn.co.uk
www.trout-inn.co.uk
2 £130 /3 £130 (£85)
1 £160
O DRY Most major cards
★★★★ All rooms en-suite

Rushey Lock *Closed Nov-March*

The Lock Keeper
Tadpole Bridge, Buckland Marsh,
Faringdon SN7 8RF
T: 01367 870218 www.environment-agency.gov.uk/homeandleisure
5 £8 WC
No vehicle access to site. Phone to book and for prices. Dogs must be kept on leads.

BUCKLAND

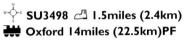 **SU3498** 🏕 **1.5miles (2.4km)**
🚂 **Oxford 14miles (22.5km)PF**

S M T W T F S   S M T W T F S

Pub: Lamb 01367 870484

B&B SC   Ashtree Farmhouse

Mrs Patricia Elliott
Buckland, Faringdon SN7 8PX
T: 01367 870540 **M:** 07971 207188
E: info@ashtree-farm.co.uk
www.ashtree-farm.co.uk
🛏 3 £85 🛏 1 £85 (£65) V 🍎 O
DRY 🔘 🚗 🚶 📶 VISA All major cards
★★★★ All rooms en-suite
🅼 VisitEngland Gold Award. Also self-
catering unit (with 2 doubles/twins),
£456 for weekend. Min age children 12
yrs. ★★★★★

⛺ Shifford Lock   *Closed Nov-end March or Easter if earlier*

The Lock Keeper
Chimney, Bampton OX18 2EJ
T: 01367 870247 www.environment-
agency.gov.uk/homeandleisure
⛺ 5 £8 🚽 🚿 🔥 🚻 📖 DRY 📶
🅼 No vehicle access to site. Phone to
book and for prices. Dogs must be kept
on leads. Camping hammocks £14.

LONGWORTH

 **SU3999** 🏕 **1.2miles (2km)**
🚂 **Oxford 11.5miles (18.5km)**

S M T W T F S   S M T W T F S

Pubs: Blue Boar 01865 820494 & Lamb
and Flag 01865 820208

Morlands   *Closed 25, 26 Dec & New Year*   B&B

Ms Fiona Benbow
High Street, Longworth, Abingdon
OX13 5DU
T: 01865 820214 **M:** 07813 787075
E: fiona@benbows.net
www.morlandsbedandbreakfast.com
🛏 1 £90 🛏 1 £80 (£65) 🚻 V 🍎
● DRY 🔘 🚗 🚶 📶 Some rooms
en-suite.

NEWBRIDGE

 **SP4001** 🏕 **on path**
🚂 **Oxford 11.5miles (18.5km)**

S M T W T F S   S M T W T F S

Pubs: Maybush 01865 300624 (closed until
May 2013) & Rose Revived 01865 300221

Rose Revived   🏨

Ms Karen Lockley
Newbridge, Witney OX29 7QD
T: 01865 300221
E: 5284@greeneking.co.uk
www.rose-revived-inn-newbridge.co.uk
🛏 5 £63 🛏 1 £58 (£58) 🛏 1 £89
🚻 🍴 V 🔥 🚭 O DRY 📶 VISA Most
major cards. Some rooms en-suite

45

Section 4

Newbridge to Oxford

The River Thames has grown to a respectable size by the time it leaves Newbridge and is usually pretty well used by a range of boats. The Thames Path along this 14 miles (22km) stretch is still remote and amazingly rural right until the centre of Oxford is reached.

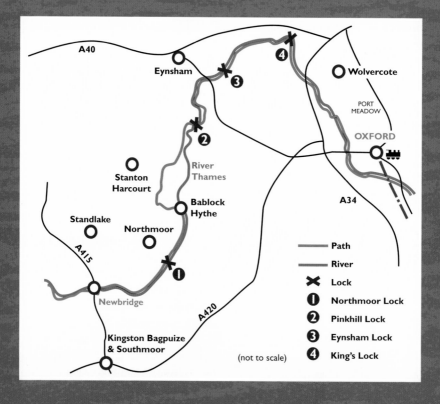

A40

Eynsham

3 Wolvercote

PORT MEADOW

OXFORD

River Thames

2

Stanton Harcourt

Bablock Hythe

A34

Standlake

Northmoor

A415

1

Newbridge

A420

Kingston Bagpuize & Southmoor

(not to scale)

Path

River

✖ Lock

1 Northmoor Lock

2 Pinkhill Lock

3 Eynsham Lock

4 King's Lock

Maps

Landranger maps	164	Oxford
Explorer maps	180	Oxford

Taxi Services

Place	Name	Telephone numbers
Southmoor	Southmoor Taxis	01865 820984
Oxford	001 Taxis	01865 240000
	A1 Taxis	01865 248000
	ABC Taxis	01865 770077/770681
	City Cars	01865 794000
	Metro Taxis	01865 777770
	Radio Taxis	01865 242424
	Royal Cars	01865 777333

Car Parking

The following is a list of public car parks close to the Thames Path and does not include on-street parking in villages or towns. Where there are several car parks in a town/city, those closest to the Path have been listed. Unfortunately theft from vehicles parked in the countryside does occasionally occur, so please leave valuables you don't want to carry at home.

Place	Map Grid Reference
Wolvercote	SP 487095
Oxford, Port Meadow	SP 502074
Oxford City Centre, various	

Newbridge

47

Toilets (♿) & 👤 and Water Points at Locks 🚰

Place	Map Grid Reference
Northmoor Lock (♿) 🚰	SP 432021
Pinkhill Lock (♿) 🚰	SP 441072
Eynsham Lock (♿) 👤 🚰	SP 445086
King's Lock 🚰	SP 479103
Wolvercote (♿)	SP 487095
Oxford, various (♿) 👤	

Visitor Information Centres

*Offers accommodation booking service for personal callers during opening hours.

Place	Address/Opening Hours
*Witney	3 Welch Way, Witney OX28 6JH
	T: 01993 775802
	E: witney.vic@westoxon.gov.uk
	www.oxfordhsirecotswolds.org
	Opening hours:
	All year: Mon-Fri 9:00-17:00; Sat 9:30-17:00
*Oxford	15-16 Broad Street, Oxford OX1 3AS
	T: 01865 252200
	www.visitoxfordandoxfordshire.com
	Opening hours:
	Summer: Mon-Sat 9:30-17:30; Sun/Bank holidays 10:00-16:00
	Winter: Mon-Sat 9:30-17:00; Sun/Bank holidays 10:00-15:00
	Closed 25-26 Dec & 1 Jan

STANDLAKE

SP3903 🚶 1mile (1.8km)
🚌 Oxford 13.7miles (22km)

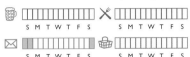

Pubs: Black Horse 01865 300307 & Bell 01865 300784

☆ Hardwick Parks Leisure park with variety of activities available
T: 01865 300501
www.hardwickparks.co.uk

🛖 Lincoln Farm Park *Closed mid Nov-Feb*

The Manager
High Street, Standlake OX29 7RH
T: 01865 300239
E: info@lincolnfarmpark.co.uk
www.lincolnfarmpark.co.uk
🛖/🚐 90 from £18 🔌 🛁 🚿 ♿
♿WC 🚽 DRY 🔘 🎲 CG 📶 📧 Most
major cards and Paypal ★★★★★

B&B The Cottage

Mrs Janice Kitchen
Witney Road, Brighthampton, Standlake OX29 7QQ
T: 01865 300891
E: info@cottagebedandbreakfastwitney.co.uk
www.cottagebedandbreakfastwitney.co.uk
🛏 2 £80 (£55) 🛏 1 £55 ♟ (min age 16) 🔌 V 🚲 🍴 ● DRY 🔘 🚗 🚶 📶
★★★★ Some rooms en-suite.
🏅 VisitEngland Gold & Breakfast Awards. Lift available to local pub.

🛖 Hardwick Parks *Closed Nov-Mar*

Downs Road, Standlake OX29 7PZ
T: 01865 300501
E: info@hardwickparks.co.uk
www.hardwickparks.co.uk
🛖/🚐 214 £16 🔌 🛁 🚿 🍴 ♿WC
🚽 🔘 🎲 CG 📧 Most major cards
★★★
🏅 7 static holiday caravans available.

KINGSTON BAGPUIZE AND SOUTHMOOR

SU4098 🚶 2.2miles (3.5km)
🚌 Oxford 9.6miles (15.5km)

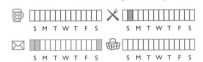

Visit www.kbsonline.org.uk for further details.
Pubs: Hinds Head 01865 820204
Waggon and Horses 01865 820230

☆ Kingston Bagpuize House and Tearoom **T:** 01865 820217

Fallowfields Country House Hotel 🏠

Mrs Peta Lloyd
Faringdon Road, Kingston Bagpuize with Southmoor OX13 5BH
T: 01865 820416
E: stay@fallowfields.com
www.fallowfields.com
🛏 6 £120 🛏 2 £120 (£95) 🛏 2
£140 ♟ 🔌 V 🚲 🌕 🍴 ● DRY 🔘
🚗 🚶 📶 📧 Most major cards
★★★ All rooms en-suite.
🏅 VisitEngland Silver Award

NORTHMOOR

 **SP4202** 1mile (1.8km)
 Oxford 14miles (22.5km)

S M T W T F S   S M T W T F S

Pub: Red Lion 01865 300301

**B&B
SC**   **Rectory Farm B&B
& Holiday Cottages**

Mrs Mary Anne Florey
Northmoor, Witney OX29 5SX
T: 01865 300207 **M:** 07974 102198
E: PJ.Florey@farmline.com
www.oxtowns.co.uk/rectoryfarm
1 £86 1 £86 (£63) V
O DRY ⏢ ⏢ Mastercard & Visa. All
rooms en-suite
B&B closed mid Dec to mid Jan.
Charges for credit card and laundry.
Self-catering accommodation ★★★★
open all year and for all ages. Prices
from £350/week.

B&B   **Westview**

Mrs Leigh Winder
Northmoor, Witney OX29 5AX
T: 01865 300741 **M:** 07973 830369
E: leigh@peterwinder.net
www.my1stweb.com/westview
/ 2 £65 (£45) V O
DRY
Order packed lunch when booking.

BABLOCK HYTHE

 **SP4304** on path
 Oxford 5.8miles (9.3km)

S M T W T F S   S M T W T F S

Pub: Ferryman Inn 01865 880028.

The Ferryman Inn

The Manager
Bablock Hythe, Northmoor OX29 5AT
T: 01865 880028
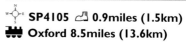 3 £65 3 £65 (£45) 1
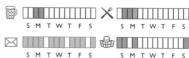 £85 V ⏢ VISA Most major cards. All
rooms en-suite.

STANTON HARCOURT

SP4105 0.9miles (1.5km)
Oxford 8.5miles (13.6km)

S M T W T F S   S M T W T F S

S M T W T F S   S M T W T F S

Shop & Post Office in Harcourt Arms
Pub: Harcourt Arms 01865 881931

EYNSHAM

 SP4309 **0.9miles (1.5km)**
Coombe 4.7miles (7.5km)

Small town with full range of services;
visit www.eynsham.org for further
details

 Talbot Inn

Mr Trevor Johnson
Oxford Road, Eynsham OX29 4BT
T: 01865 881348
M: 07787 524370
E: enquiries@talbot-oxford.co.uk
www.talbot-oxford.co.uk

2 £75 6 £75 2 £85 3
£40 ⚭ 🔌 ▼ 🔥 🌙 🔵 ⚪ 🔵 ⏶ 🐕
📶 💳 Most major cards ★★★Some
rooms en-suite.

 White Hart

Mr Russell Trotman
31 Newland Street, Eynsham OX29 4LB
T: 01865 880711
E: whiteharteynsham@btconnect.com
www.whiteharteynsham.co.uk

2 £54 1 £54 (£42) ⚭ 🔌
▼ 🔥 🌙 🔵 ⚪ 🔵 🚗 🐕 📶 💳
Most major cards. All rooms en-suite.
🍴 No evening meal Sundays & Mondays.

Pinkhill Lock *Closed Nov-31st March*

The Lock Keeper
Eynsham OX29 4JH
T: 01865 881452 www.environment-
agency.gov.uk/homeandleisure
⛺ 5 £8 🔌 🔥 🌙 🔵 🚻 💳 Most
major cards
🍴 No vehicle access to site. Phone to
book and for prices. Dogs must be kept
on leads. Small fires allowed.

Eynsham Lock *Closed Nov-end March*

The Lock Keeper
Swinford Bridge, Eynsham OX29 4BY
T: 01865 881324 www.environment-
agency.gov.uk/homeandleisure
⛺ 10 £5.50 🔌 🔥 🌙 🚻 ♿WC 📄
💳 Most major cards
🍴 Also open at Easter. No vehicle
access to site. Phone to book and for
prices. Dogs must be kept on leads.

WOLVERCOTE

 SP4809 **0.5miles (0.8km)**
Oxford 3.4miles (5.5km) 🚻

OXFORD

⌖ **SP5106** 👣 **on path**

🚂 **Oxford**

City with full range of services, museums, colleges and other attractions. Visit www. visitoxfordandoxfordshire.com for further details. Oxford has a wide range of accommodation – details from Visitor Information Centre (see section introduction).

Oxford YHA ▲

The Manager
2A Botley Road, Oxford OX2 0AB
T: 01865 727275
E: oxford@yha.org.uk
www.yha.org.uk

🛏 5 🛏 5 🛏 30 👤 | ♟ ♿ V 🔥
🅥 ⓘ Ⓞ DRY 🔯 VISA Most major cards
★★★★ Some rooms en-suite
🍴 Prices from £15 per person.

Oxford Camping & Caravanning Site ⛺

The Manager
426 Abingdon Road, Oxford OX1 4XG
T: 01865 244088
www.campingandcaravanningclub.co.uk
⛺ 43 £7 🚐 42 £8 🔲 🔧 🚿 Ⓜ 🔳
🔯 CG VISA Most major cards

🍴 Prices are for low season for members. Non-members are welcome

Radcliffe Camera, Oxford

Section 5

Oxford to Abingdon

This relatively short section of 10 miles (16km) is still essentially rural once the Thames Path has left the centre of Oxford striking south.

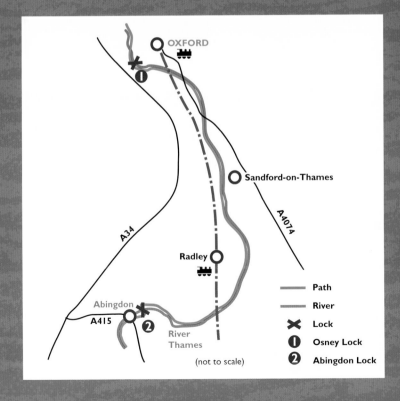

OXFORD

Sandford-on-Thames

A4074

A34

Radley

Abingdon

A415

River Thames

Path

River

✖ Lock

❶ Osney Lock

❷ Abingdon Lock

(not to scale)

Maps

Landranger maps	164	Oxford
Explorer maps	180	Oxford
	170	Abingdon, Wantage & Vale of White Horse

Taxi Services

Place	Name	Telephone numbers
Oxford	001 Taxis	01865 240000
	A1 Taxis	01865 248000
	ABC Taxis	01865 770077/770681
	City Cars	01865 794000
	Metro Taxis	01865 777770
	Radio Taxis	01865 242424
	Royal Cars	01865 777333
Abingdon	Abicabs	01235 423268
	Auto Taxis	01235 527711/555735
	Broe K Cabs	01235 524999
	Su's Taxis	01235 554085
	Toots Taxis	01235 555599
	Vargas Taxis	01235 559606

Car Parking

The following is a list of public car parks close to the Thames Path and does not include on-street parking in villages or towns. Where there are several car parks in a town, those closest to the Path have been listed. Unfortunately theft from vehicles parked in the countryside does occasionally occur, so please leave valuables you don't want to carry at home.

Place	Map Grid Reference
Oxford, Port Meadow	SP 502074
Oxford City Centre, various	
Abingdon, Rye Farm, on A415 south of Abingdon Bridge	SU 501967
Abingdon, Hales Meadow car park, downstream side of bridge	SU 500967

Toilets ⓦ & ♿ and Water Points at Locks 🚰

Place	Map Grid Reference
Oxford, various ⓦ ♿	
Osney Lock 🚰	SP 503059
Abingdon Lock ⓦ Men's only 🚰	SU 506971
Abingdon, Hales Meadow car park, downstream side of bridge ⓦ ♿	SU 500967

Visitor Information Centres

* Offers accommodation booking service for personal callers during opening hours.

Place	Address/Opening Hours
*Oxford	15-16 Broad Street, Oxford OX1 3AS **T**: 01865 252200 www.visitoxfordandoxfordshire.com **Opening hours:** Summer: Mon-Sat 9:30-17:30; Sun/Bank holidays 10:00-16:00 Winter: Mon-Sat 9:30-17:00; Sun/Bank holidays 10:00-15:00 Closed 25-26 Dec & 1 Jan
*Abingdon	Visitor & Community Information Centre, Old Abbey House, Abbey Close, Abingdon OX14 3JD **T**: 01235 522711 www.visitvale.com **Opening hours:** All Year: Mon-Fri 9:00-17:15; Tues-Fri 9:00-17:00; Sat 10:00-15:00

Fiddler's Island, Oxford, upstream of Osney Bridge

55

SANDFORD-ON-THAMES

⊕ SP5301 🛶 on path
🚂 Oxford 4.7miles (7.5km)

🍺 |||||||||||| ✕ ||||||||||||
S M T W T F S   S M T W T F S

Pubs: Kings Arms 01865 777095 & Catherine
Wheel 01865 778340

Ⓗ

Reservations
Henley Road, Sandford-on-Thames OX4
4GX
T: 01865 334400
E: thames@four-pillars.co.uk
http://oxford-thames-hotel.four-pillars.
co.uk
🛏 84 £130 (£115) 🕴 ♿ V 🔥
🚫 **DRY** 📷 📶 **VISA** Most major cards
★★★★ All rooms en-suite
🅷 No evening meals in December.

RADLEY

⊕ SP5299 🛶 0.9miles (1.5km)
🚂 Radley

🍺 |||||||||||| ✕ ||||||||||||
S M T W T F S   S M T W T F S

✉ |||||||||||| 🧺 ||||||||||||
S M T W T F S   S M T W T F S

🅰 In post office
Pub: Bowyer Arms 01235 523452

ABINGDON

⊕ SU4997 🛶 on path
🚂 Radley 2.2miles (3.5km)

Town with full range of services, visit
www.abingdon.gov.uk for further details.
It has a wide range of accommodation
– details from Visitor Information
Centre (see section introduction).

☆ Kingscraft and Abingdon Boat Centre
T: 01235 521125

☆ Abingdon Abbey **T:** 01235 525339

☆ Abingdon Museum **T:** 01235 523703
www.abingdonmuseum.org.uk

Abingdon Bridge

Section 6

Abingdon to Wallingford

It is during this 13¹/₂ miles (22km) section that settlements start to become more frequent, for as well as starting and finishing in historic towns, several villages are encountered on or close to the Thames Path. However, in between the countryside remains generally quiet.

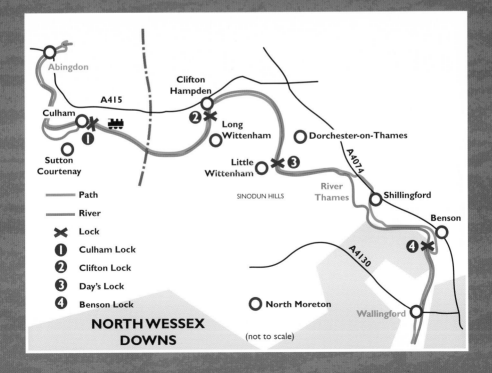

Abingdon

A415

Culham

Clifton Hampden

Long Wittenham

❷✖

Dorchester-on-Thames

Little Wittenham ✖❸

Sutton Courtenay

❶✖🚂

SINODUN HILLS

River Thames

A4074

Shillingford

Benson

A4130

❹✖

North Moreton

Wallingford

Path

River

✖ Lock

❶ Culham Lock

❷ Clifton Lock

❸ Day's Lock

❹ Benson Lock

NORTH WESSEX DOWNS

(not to scale)

Maps

Landranger maps	164	Oxford
	175	Reading & Windsor
Explorer maps	180	Oxford

Taxi Services

Place	Name	Telephone numbers
Abingdon	Abicabs	01235 423268
	Auto Taxis	01235 527711/555735
	Broe K Cabs	01235 524999
	Su's Taxis	01235 554085
	Toots Taxis	01235 555599
	Vargas Taxis	01235 559606
Clifton Hampden	Clifton Cars	01865 407076
Wallingford	Hills Taxis	01491 837022

Car Parking

The following is a list of public car parks close to the Thames Path and does not include on-street parking in villages or towns. Where there are several car parks in a town, those closest to the Path have been listed. Unfortunately theft from vehicles parked in the countryside does occasionally occur, so please leave valuables you don't want to carry at home.

Place	Map Grid Reference
Abingdon, Rye Farm, on A415 south of Abingdon Bridge	SU 501967
Abingdon, Hales Meadow car park, downstream side of bridge	SU 500967
Culham Lock	SU 507949
Clifton Hampden bridge, south of river opposite Barley Mow pub	SU 548953
Wallingford Riverside, east of the river	SU 612895

Toilets (†) & ♿ and Water Points at Locks ⚰

Place	Map Grid Reference
Abingdon Lock (†) Men's only ⚰	SU 506971
Abingdon, Hales Meadow car park, downstream side of bridge (†) ♿	SU 500967
Culham Lock (†) ⚰	SU 507949
Clifton Lock ⚰	SU 547947
Day's Lock (†)	SU 569936
Benson Lock ⚰	SU 613913
Wallingford, Cattle Market car park, Wood Street (†) ♿	SU 608893
Wallingford, Riverside (†) ♿ (March-Sept)	SU 612896
Wallingford, St Albans car park, off High Street (†) ♿	SU 606895

Visitor Information Centres

* Offers accommodation booking service for personal callers during opening hours.

Place	Address/Opening Hours
*Abingdon	Visitor & Community Information Centre, Old Abbey House, Abbey Close, Abingdon OX14 3JD **T**: 01235 522711 www.visitvale.com **Opening hours:** All Year: Mon-Fri 9:00-17:15; Tues-Fri 9:00-17:00; Sat 10:00-15:00
*Wallingford	Town Hall, Market Place, Wallingford OX10 0EG. **T**: 01491 826972 **E**: wallingfordtic@btconnect.com www.wallingford.co.uk **Opening hours:** Mar-Mid Dec: Mon-Fri 10:00-16:00, Sat 10:00-14:00 Mid Dec-Feb: Mon-Sat 10:00-14:00

CULHAM

 **SU5095** 👢 **on path**
🚂 **Culham 1.6miles (2.5km) PF**

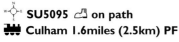
S M T W T F S   S M T W T F S

Pubs: Waggon & Horses 01235 525012
& Railway Inn 01235 528046

 Tel: 01235 521777
www.zouchfarm.co.uk

★★★★

Zouch Farm is a 750 acre, mainly arable working farm with beautiful views and a tranquil setting.

Our 3 ensuite rooms are spacious and inviting with king size beds.

All breakfasts are cook-to-order and use locally sourced ingredients, where possible.

Zouch Farm   B&B

Mrs Selina Wallis
Culham, Abingdon OX14 3BS
T: 01235 521777 **M:** 07811 364497
E: selina_wallis@hotmail.co.uk
www.zouchfarm.co.uk
🛏 3 £95 (£75) 🚼 📺 V 🐾 ● DRY 🖥
🚗 🛜 VISA All major cards ★★★★
All rooms en-suite
H VisitEngland Silver & Breakfast awards

Railway Inn

Mrs Pauline Davidson
Station Road, Culham OX14 3BT
T: 01235 528046
E: info@railwayinnculham.co.uk
www.railwayinnculham.co.uk
🛏 4 £68 🛏 3 £68 (£50) 🛏 2 £90
🚼 ♿ 📺 V 🐾 🍸 ● DRY 🚗 🛜 VISA
Most major cards ★★★ All rooms en-suite

SUTTON COURTENAY

 **SU5093** 👢 **0.9miles (1.5km)**
🚂 **Didcot 3.4miles (5.5km) PF**

S M T W T F S   S M T W T F S

S M T W T F S   S M T W T F S

In post office
Pubs: George & Dragon 01235 848142
& Fish 01235 848242

Railway Inn

Tel: 01235 528046

www.railwayinnculham.co.uk

A traditional English inn offering real ales, delicious home cooked food and comfortable bed & breakfast accommodation. The inn is adjacent to the Oxford Paddington line at Culham Station. Easy access to the A34, M40 and M4 by car.

B&B Appletree Cottage

Mrs Moira Worrell
5 Appleford Road, Sutton Courtenay
OX14 4NG
T: 01235 848071
E: bob@appletreecottage-bb.co.uk
www.appletreecottage-bb.co.uk

🛏 1 £45 🛏 3 £45 (£30) 🛏 1 £55
👪 (min age 1) ♿ 📺 V ☕ ⚫ DRY 🐾
📶 All rooms en-suite

The Courtyard   *Closed Xmas* B&B

Ms Sue Cornwall
All Saints Lane, Sutton Courtenay
OX14 4AG
T: 01235 848888
E: susancornwall@aol.com

🛏 1 £85 🛏 1 £85 (£45) 👪 ♿ V
🐾 ☕ ⚫ DRY 📻 🐾 📶 VISA Paypal. All rooms en-suite

CLIFTON HAMPDEN

🧭 **SU5495** 👢 on path
🚂 **Culham 1.1miles (1.8km)**

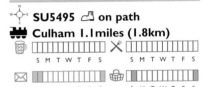

🍺 | | | | | | | | | | | | | ✕ | | | | | | | | | | | |
  S M T W T F S   S M T W T F S

✉ | | | | | | | | | | | | 🛒 | | | | | | | | | | | |
  S M T W T F S   S M T W T F S

Pubs: Plough Inn 01865 407699 & Barley Mow 01865 407847

Bridge House Caravan Site   *Closed Nov- March* ⛺

Miss E Gower
Bridge House, Clifton Hampden,
OX14 3EH
T: 01865 407725
⛺/🚐 24 £12 📺 🚿 🚰 ♿ 📱 ⚫
🚫 No children allowed. Caravan hire £195/week.

Plough Inn

Mrs Mary Ya
Abingdon Road, Clifton Hampden
OX14 3EG
T: 01865 407699 **M:** 07718 585200
E: maryya@hotmail.co.uk
www.theploughinns.com
6 £78 V 🌙 🛜 💳 Most major
cards. All rooms en-suite
🍴 Restaurant closed Sundays in winter

LONG WITTENHAM

SU5493 ⛺ 1.6miles (2.5km)
🚂 Culham 2.4miles (3.8km)

S M T W T F S   S M T W T F S

Pubs: Plough 01865 407738 &
Vine & Spice Inn 01865 409900

☆ Pendon Museum of Miniature
Landscape and Transport - open 14:00-
16:45 weekends **T:** 01865 407365
www.pendonmuseum.com

B&B **The Grange**

Mr Graham Neil
Long Wittenham, Abingdon OX14 4QH
T: 01865 407808 **M:** 07831 581544
E: graham@grangebb.com
2 £55 2 £55 (£45) 🧍 (min
age 8) V 🐾 🍎 ● DRY 📷 🚗 🚶 🛜
★★★★ Some rooms en-suite

Witta's Ham Cottage   *Closed Xmas*   B&B

Mrs Jill Mellor
High Street, Long Wittenham, Abingdon
OX14 4QH
T: 01865 407686
E: jill@wittenham.com
1 £70 1 £70 (£50) 🧍 (min
age 4) 🔌 V 🐾 🍎 O DRY 📷 🚗 🚶
🛜 Some rooms en-suite

LITTLE WITTENHAM

SU5693 ⛺ on opposite bank
of river
🚂 Culham 3.5miles (5.6km)

☆ Little Wittenham Nature Reserve,
Wittenham Clumps and Earth Trust
T: 01865 407792 www.earthtrust.org.uk

Day's Lock   *Closed Oct - Easter*

The Lock Keeper
Day's Lock, Little Wittenham, Abingdon
OX14 4RB
T: 01865 407768 www.environment-
agency.gov.uk/homeandleisure
⛺ 5 £8 🔌 🚲 🎣 (🅟) 🚻
🍴 No vehicle access to site. Phone to
book. Dogs must be kept on leads.

Keepers Cottage   B&B

John and Julia Sargent
6 Hillside, Little Wittenham, Abingdon
OX14 4QX
T: 01865 407922
E: julia.sargent@little-wittenham.co.uk
1 £65 1 £65 (£40) V 🐾 🌙 🍎
O DRY 🚗 🚶 🛜 Twin room en-suite
🍴 Double room has private bathroom

North Moreton

SU5689 🥾 **2.8miles (4.4km)**
🚆 **Didcot 3miles (4.8km)**

🍺 |||||||||||||| ✕ |||||||||||||
S M T W T F S   S M T W T F S

Pub: Bear at Home 01235 811311.
In winter closed Sunday evenings

B&B
SC

Haddon Acre

Mrs Susan Hollebone
Sires Hill, North Moreton OX11 9BG
T: 01235 812052 **M:** 07721 364212
E: sue@hollebone.com
www.haddonacre.co.uk
🛏/🛏 1 £85 (£65) & **DRY** 🚗
🧍 📶 💳 Most major cards & Paypal.
Room is en-suite
⚓ Lift provided to local pub and
supermarket. Self catering Mongolian
yurt with log cabin £80 per night

Purple loosestrife

Dorchester-on-Thames

SU5794 🥾 **1.2miles (2km)**
🚆 **Culham 4miles (6.5km)**

Small town with range of services, visit
www.dorchester-on-thames.co.uk for
further details

☆ Dorchester Abbey, Museum and Tea
Room
T: 01865 340007
www.dorchester-abbey.org.uk

☆ Hurst Water Meadow
www.hurst-water-meadow.co.uk

George Hotel

Mr Liaan Van Zyl
High Street, Dorchester-on-Thames
OX10 7HH
T: 01865 340304
E: georgedorchester@relaxinnz.co.uk
www.thegeorgedorchester.co.uk
🛏 17 £85 🛏 5 £85 🛏 2 £75 👫 &
V 🏍 🚱 🍎 **DRY** 📱 🧍 📶 💳 All major
cards ★★★All rooms en-suite
⚓ Contact for details of special
midweek rates for walkers.

White Hart Hotel

Mr Sean Harris
High Street, Dorchester-on-Thames
OX10 7HN
T: 01865 340074
E: whitehart@oxfordshire-hotels.co.uk
www.white-hart-hotel-dorchester.co.uk
🛏/🛏 26 £105 (£95) 🛏 2 £95 👫
& 📱 V 🏍 🚱 🍎 ● 📱 📶 💳 Most
major cards ★★★ All rooms en-suite

SHILLINGFORD

SU5992 🥾 **on path**
🚂 **Cholsey 5.2miles (8.3km)**

🍺 |||||||||| ✕ ||||||||||
   S M T W T F S   S M T W T F S

Pub: Shillingford Bridge Hotel 01865
858567

B&B Alouette

Mrs Wendy Seymour
2 Caldicott Close, Shillingford OX10 7HF
T: 01865 858600 **M:** 07717 747454
E: wendy@alouettebandb.co.uk
www.alouettebandb.co.uk
🛏 1 £55 🛏 1 £55 (£45) 🛏 2 £45
⛹ (min age 12) V 🧖 🜜 ♿ O DRY 🔲 🚗
🐾 🛜 ★★★★ Some rooms en-suite
🅽 VisitEngland Silver & Breakfast
awards.

Kingfisher Inn

Mr Alexis Somarakis
27 Henley Road, Shillingford OX10 7EL
T: 01865 858595
E: guestrooms@kingfisher-inn.co.uk
www.kingfisher-inn.co.uk
🛏 5 £95 🛏 1 £95 (£70) 🛏 6
£70 ⛹ V 🧖 🜜 ♿ O DRY 🐾 🛜 VISA
Most major cards ★★★★ All rooms
en-suite

Marsh House   B&B

Mrs Patricia Nickson
7 Court Drive, Shillingford OX10 7ER
T: 01865 858496
E: marsh.house@talk21.com
www.marshhousebandb.co.uk
🛏 1 £75 🛏 1 £75 (£50) 🛏 1 £45
⛹ (min age 8) V 🧖 🜜 O DRY 🚗 🐾
🛜 ★★★★ All rooms en-suite

Shillingford Bridge Hotel

Mr Robert Carr
Shillingford Hill, Wallingford OX10 8LZ
T: 01865 858567
E: shillingford.bridge@forestdale.com
www.shillingfordbridgehotel.com
🛏 22 £65 🛏 8 £65 🛏 10 £55 ⛹
♿ 🜜 V 🧖 🜜 🜜 O DRY 🔲 🛜 VISA All
major cards ★★★ All rooms en-suite

Bridge House   B&B

Philip and Rosemary Mader-Grayson
72 Wallingford Road, Shillingford OX10 7EU
T: 01865 858540
E: house@bridge-house.org.uk
www.bridge-house.org.uk
🛏 2 £55 🛏 1 £55 (£40) ⛹ 🜜
V 🧖 🜜 🜜 ● DRY 🔲 🐾 All rooms
en-suite

⛺ 10+ from £6 🚐 5 £12 🜜 🜜 🜜
🅧 ♿ WC 🔲 DRY 🔲 VISA Paypal
🅽 Farm shop on site. Camping closed
Oct-Easter.

BENSON

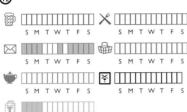

SU6191 🥾 **on path**

🚂 **Cholsey 5.1miles (8.2km) P F**

♿

[schedule bars]

S M T W T F S   S M T W T F S

S M T W T F S   S M T W T F S

S M T W T F S   S M T W T F S

S M T W T F S

🔲 At service station and off-licence

Pubs: Crown Inn 01491 838247 & Three Horseshoes 01491 838242

☆ Salters Steamers
T: 01865 243421
www.salterssteamers.co.uk

Benson Waterfront *Closed Nov-March*

Mr Adrian Tilbury
Benson OX10 6SJ
T: 01491 838304
E: sales@bensonwaterfront.co.uk
www.bensonwaterfront.com
⛺ 6 £20 🚐 16 £20 🔲 ♨ 🚰 ♿
♿WC 🔲 DRY 🔲 💳 Most major cards
🍴 On site cafe/bistro.

Brookside *Closed Xmas* B&B

Mrs Jill Folley
Brook Street, Benson OX10 6LJ
T: 01491 838289 **M:** 07979 813302
E: clivefolley@btinternet.com
🛏 1 £60 (£40) 🛏 1 £90 👪 🔲 V 🍎
○ DRY �car ♿ 📶 All rooms en-suite
🍴 Breakfast £5/person extra

Crown Inn INN

Mrs Petra Smith
52 High Street, Benson OX10 6RP
T: 01491 838247
E: crowninnbenson@sky.com
www.crowninnbenson.co.uk
🛏 3 £50 🛏 1 £50 🛏 1 £65 🛏
1 £30 👪 🔲 V ♨ 🔲 🍷 ○ 🔲 📶 💳
Most major cards. All rooms en-suite.
🍴 All prices exclude breakfast. No evening meals Sundays & Mondays.

Fyfield Manor B&B

Mrs Christine Brown
Benson OX10 6HA
T: 01491 835184 **M:** 07779 722202
E: chris_fyfield@hotmail.co.uk
www.fyfieldmanor.co.uk
🛏 1 £80 🛏 1 £80 (£55) 🛏 1
£100 👪 (min age 10) V ♨ 🍎● DRY
🚗 📶 💳 Most major cards. All rooms en-suite.

WALLINGFORD

SU6089 🥾 **on path**
🚆 **Cholsey 2.9miles (4.7km)**
Town with full range of services, visit
www.wallingford.co.uk for further
details.

☆ Wallingford Museum
T: 01491 835065
www.wallingfordmuseum.org.uk

☆ Wallingford Castle and Meadows

Ⓗ George Hotel

Mr Oliver Round-Turner
High Street, Wallingford OX10 0BS
T: 01491 836665
E: rooms@george-hotel-wallingford.com
www.george-hotel-wallingford.com
🛏️ 12 £110 🛏️ 23 £110 (£90) 🛏️ 2
£140 🛏️ 8 £90 ♟(min age 1) ♿ V 🔥
🐾 ⬤ 🅾️ DRY 📶 💳 Most major cards
★★★ All rooms en-suite

52 Blackstone Road   B&B

Mrs Enid Barnard
52 Blackstone Road, Wallingford OX10
8JL
T: 01491 839339
E: enid.barnard@googlemail.com
🛏️ 1 £45 (£35) 🛏️ 1 £23 🐾 V ⬤ 🅾️
DRY 🚗 👣 📶

Old School House   B&B
Closed 2 weeks at Xmas

Mrs Carolyn Bristow
23 Castle Street, Wallingford OX10
8DW
T: 01491 839571 **M:** 07900 225167
E: bristow.carolyn@gmail.com
www.23oldschoolhouse.com
🛏️ 2 £75 ♟ (min age 10) V 🍎
⬤ DRY 👣 📶 💳 Paypal. All rooms
en-suite

Wallingford Bridge

Section 7

Wallingford to Tilehurst

These 15 miles (24km) of the Thames Path finishing on the outskirts of Reading provide contrasting landscapes and some lovely settlements. Firstly there's open countryside with wide views but before long the River Thames is squeezed between hills as it passes through the Goring Gap with the wooded Chilterns as a backdrop.

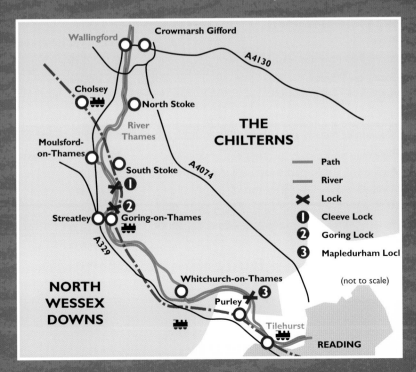

Wallingford

Crowmarsh Gifford

A4130

Cholsey

North Stoke

River Thames

THE CHILTERNS

Moulsford-on-Thames

South Stoke ❶

A4074

Streatley ❷ Goring-on-Thames

A329

Whitchurch-on-Thames

Purley ❸

Tilehurst

NORTH WESSEX DOWNS

READING

— Path

— River

✖ Lock

❶ Cleeve Lock

❷ Goring Lock

❸ Mapledurham Locl

(not to scale)

Maps

Landranger maps	175	Reading & Windsor
	174	Newbury & Wantage
Explorer maps	171	Chiltern Hills West

Taxi Services

Place	Name	Telephone numbers
Wallingford	Hills Taxis	01491 837022
Goring-on-Thames	Asa Cars	01491 521668
	Chrissie's Cabs	01491 682412/07808 162958
	Murdock Taxis	01491 872029

Car Parks

The following is a list of public car parks close to the Thames Path and does not include on-street parking in villages or towns. Where there are several car parks in a town, those closest to the Path have been listed. Unfortunately theft from vehicles parked in the countryside does occasionally occur, so please leave valuables you don't want to carry at home.

Place	Map Grid Reference
Wallingford Riverside, east of the river	SU 612895
Goring-on-Thames	SU 599807
Pangbourne, south side of bridge	SU 636767

Toilets ⊛ & ♿ and Water Points at Locks 🚰

Place	Map Grid Reference
Wallingford, Cattle Market car park, Wood Street ⊛ ♿	SU 608893
Wallingford, Riverside ⊛ ♿ (Mar-Sep)	SU 612896
Wallingford St Albans car park, off High Street ⊛ ♿	SU 606895
Cleeve Lock, upstream of Goring-on-Thames ⊛ 🚰	SU 601818
Goring Lock 🚰	SU 598809
Goring-on-Thames car park ⊛ ♿	SU 599807
Pangbourne, Riverside Meadow ⊛ ♿	SU 636767
Mapledurham Lock ⊛ ♿ 🚰	SU 667768

Visitor Information Centres

* Offers accommodation booking service for personal callers during opening hours.

Place

*Wallingford

Address/Opening Hours

Town Hall, Market Place, Wallingford OX10 0EG.
T: 01491 826972   **E:** wallingfordtic@btconnect.com
www.wallingford.co.uk

Opening hours:
Mar-Mid Dec: Mon-Fri 10:00-16:00, Sat 10:00-14:00
Mid Dec-Feb: Mon-Sat 10:00-14:00

CROWMARSH GIFFORD

SU6191 🛏 **0.3miles (0.5km)**
🚂 **Cholsey 3.5miles (5.7km)** ☎

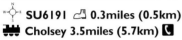

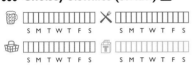

Pubs: Queen's Head 01491 839857 &
Bell/Hungry Horse 01491 835324.

B&B ### Little Gables

Mrs Carole Baker
166 Crowmarsh Hill, Wallingford OX10
8BG
T: 01491 837834
E: mail@littlegables.co.uk
www.littlegables.co.uk
🛏 3 £80 🛏 3 £80 (£65) 🛏 2
£150 🛏 4 £65 ♀♂ ▣ V 🔥🍽 ● DRY
▣ 🐕 🚗 🛜 VISA Most major cards
★★★★ Some rooms en-suite
◀ VisitEngland Silver & Breakfast
awards. 5% surcharge for credit card use.

Riverside Park & Pools
Closed Oct-Easter

Mr John Busby
The Street, Crowmarsh Gifford,
Wallingford OX10 8EB
T: 01491 835232 E: riverside@gll.org
www.better.org.uk/leisure
Å/🚐 18 £15 🔥 🔥 ⑪ ♿WC 🖥 🍽
VISA Some major cards
◀ Phone 01865 341035 out of season

Bridge Villa Camping & Caravan Park
B&B
Å

Mr Andrew Townsend
Crowmarsh Gifford, Wallingford OX10
8HB
T: 01491 836860 **M:** 07801 274116
E: bridge.villa@btinternet.com
www.bridgevilla.co.uk
🛏 1 £45 (£40) ♀♂ ♿ DRY ▣ VISA Most
major cards. Room is en-suite
Å 55 £12 🚐 56 £16 ▣ 🔥 🔥 ⑪
♿WC 🖥 DRY ▣ 🍽 CG VISA Most
major cards

NORTH STOKE

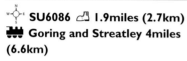 **SU6086** 1.9miles (2.7km)
Goring and Streatley 4miles (6.6km)

S M T W T F S   S M T W T F S

Pub: Springs Hotel 01491 836687

Springs Hotel & Golf Club

Mrs Helen Kennard
Wallingford Road, North Stoke,
Wallingford OX10 6BE
T: 01491 836687
E: reception@thespringshotel.com
www.thespringshotel.com

28 £110 16 £110 (£95)
3 £140 V O
Most major cards ★★★
All rooms en-suite

CHOLSEY

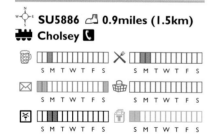 **SU5886** 0.9miles (1.5km)
Cholsey

S M T W T F S   S M T W T F S

S M T W T F S   S M T W T F S

S M T W T F S   S M T W T F S

S M T W T F S

Pubs: Morning Star 01491 651413 &
Red Lion 01491 651295

☆ Cholsey and Wallingford Railway
www.cholsey-wallingford-railway.com
T: 01491 835067

33 Ilges Lane   *Closed 25-31 Dec*   B&B

Mrs Hazel Jensen
Cholsey, Wallingford OX10 9NX
T: 01491 651974 **M:** 07880 895839
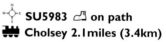 1 £45 (£30) V O DRY

MOULSFORD-ON-THAMES

 SU5983 on path
Cholsey 2.1miles (3.4km)

S M T W T F S

Restaurant: Beetle & Wedge Boathouse
01491 651381

Beetle & Wedge Boathouse   *Closed 1st week Jan*   B&B

Mrs Stephanie Musk
Ferry Lane, Moulsford OX10 9JF
T: 01491 651381
E: boathouse@beetleandwedge.co.uk
www.beetleandwedge.co.uk
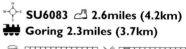 3 £90 (£75) V O
DRY Most major cards.
★★★★ All rooms en-suite
On site restaurant open daily

SOUTH STOKE

 **SU6083** 2.6miles (4.2km)
Goring 2.3miles (3.7km)

S M T W T F S   S M T W T F S

Pub: Perch and Pike 01491 872415

Perch and Pike

Mr Neil Dorsett
The Street, South Stoke RG8 0JS
T: 01491 872415
E: info@perchandpike.co.uk
www.perchandpike.co.uk/
🛏 3 £85 🚪 1 £85 ⁇ V 🔥 ◑ ⦿ 🖼
📶 💳 Most major cards. ★★★ All rooms en-suite.

B&B Oak Barn

Mrs Vanessa Guiver
The Old Post Office, The Street, South Stoke, Reading RG8 0JS
T: 01491 871872 **M:** 07889 757767
E: vanessa.guiver@btinternet.com
www.oakbarn.org
🛏 1 £80 (£50) ⁇ (min age 5) V 🔥 ◑ ● DRY 🖥 🚗 🖼 📶 Room is en-suite

STREATLEY

⊹ **SU5980** 🥾 on path
🚉 Goring and Streatley 0.7miles
(1.2km)

🍺 |||||||||||||| ✕ ||||||||||||||
  S M T W T F S   S M T W T F S

Pubs: Bull at Streatley 01491 872392 & Swan at Streatley Hotel 01491 878800. Most facilities available nearby in Goring. For further information visit www.streatley-on-thames.co.uk

Swan at Streatley

Mr Karl Bentley
High Street, Streatley RG8 9HR
T: 01491 878800
E: reception@swan-at-streatley
www.swanatstreatley.co.uk
🛏 22 £110 🚪 8 £110 (£105)
🛏 9 £95 ⁇ ♿ 🖼 V 🔥 ◑ ⦿ ○ 🖥
📶 💳 Most major cards ★★★★ All rooms en-suite
▮ VisitEngland Silver Award. Restaurant and spa on site.

3 Icknield Cottages   B&B

Mrs Susan Brodie
High Street, Streatley RG8 9JA
T: 01491 875152
🛏 1 £30 V 🔥 ◑ ● DRY 🖥 📶
▮ Private bathroom

Bull at Streatley

Emma Brooks
Reading Road, Streatley RG8 9JJ
T: 01491 872392
E: contact@bullstreatley.com
www.bullstreatley.com
🛏 4 £70 🚪 1 £80 ⁇ 🖼 V 🔥 ◑
📶 💳 Most major cards. All rooms en-suite.
▮ Breakfast not included. No meals after 7:30pm on Sundays.

B&B Stable Cottages

Mrs Diana Fenton
Streatley RG8 9JX
T: 01491 874408
🛏 I £60 (£30) 🍴 I £30 👪(min age
8) V 🏔 🛈 O DRY 🔲 🚗 🧺 🛜

▲ Streatley YHA

Mr Nick Crivich
Reading Road, Streatley RG8 9JJ
T: 01491 872278
E: streatley@yha.org.uk
www.yha.org.uk
👪(min age I) ♿ V 🏔 🛈 O DRY
🔲 Most major cards ★★★
🛏 8 rooms from £25. Disabled access
by arrangement

GORING-ON-THAMES

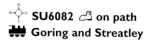 SU6082 🥾 on path
🚉 Goring and Streatley

Small town with range of services. For
information see www.goring-on-thames.
co.uk

B&B Beams End

Mrs Jean Turner
Station Road, Goring-on-Thames RG8
9HA
T: 01491 875949
E: jeanturner@btinternet.com
🛏 2 £70 V 🏔 🍎 O 🧺 🛜

Friars Ford B&B

Mrs Emma Bermingham
Manor Road, Goring-on-Thames RG8
9EL
T: 01491 872470 **M:** 07801 138410
E: bermingham.emma@gmail.com
www.friars-ford.co.uk
🛏 2 £80 🍴 I £80 (£50) 👪 V 🏔
🛈 O DRY 🚗 🧺 🛜 VISA Paypal. All
rooms en-suite.

John Barleycorn INN

Robert and Sandra Hurst
Manor Road, Goring-on-Thames RG8
9DP
T: 01491 872509
E: enquiries@thejohnbarleycornpub.co.uk
www.thejohnbarleycornpub.co.uk
🛏 3 £75 👪 V 🏔 🛈 🍺 🛜 VISA Most
major cards. All rooms en-suite
🛏 No evening meals on Sundays

Lycroft B&B

Mrs Frances Thompson
3 Lycroft Close, Goring-on-Thames
RG8 0AT
T: 01491 873052
E: francesthompson1@btinternet.com
🛏 I £60 🍴 I £30 👪 📶 V 🏔 🛈 🍺
DRY 🔲 🚗 🛜
🛏 Lift provided to pub

B&B

Mrs Rosemary Howarth
36 Milldown Road, Goring-on-Thames
RG8 0BD
T: 01491 873040 **M:** 07798 663897
E: melrose-cottage@goring-on-thames.
co.uk
🛏 2 £60 (£45) 🛏 1 £35 👫(min
age 5) **V** 🔥 🕯 O **DRY** 🔟 🚗 📶 ☰
Paypal

B&B

Mrs & Mr Dawn and Richard Roberts
Farm Road, Goring-on-Thames RG8
0AA
T: 01491 872184
E: goringbnb@rglroberts.com
🛏 2 £70 🛏 1 £70 (£60) 👫 🔳 **V**
🔥 🌑 🍎 O **DRY** 🔟 🚗 👣 📶

WHITCHURCH-ON-THAMES

🧭 **SU6377** 👢 **on path**
🚂 **Pangbourne 0.6miles (1km)**

🍺 ▥▥▥▥▥▥ ✗ ▥▥▥▥▥▥
    S M T W T F S   S M T W T F S

Pubs: Greyhound 0118 984 4800 &
Ferryboat 0118 984 2161. Visit
www.whitchurchonthames.com for
information

PANGBOURNE

🧭 **SU6376** 👢 **on path**
🚂 **Pangbourne**

Small town with range of services, visit
www.pangbourne-on-thames.com for
further details

☆ Beale Park
T: 0844 826 1761
www.bealepark.co.uk

Weir View House **B&B**

Mrs Fiona Langridge
9 Shooters Hill, Pangbourne RG8 7DZ
T: 0118 984 2120 **M:** 07791 294995
E: info@weirview.co.uk
www.weirview.co.uk
🛏 9 £90 🛏 3 £105 👫 ♿ **V** 🔥
👣 📶 ☰ Most major cards. ★★★★
All rooms en-suite
🍴 Continental breakfast only
VisitEngland Gold award.

Whitchurch-on-Thames toll bridge

PURLEY

⊕ **SU6676** 👢 **on path**
🚂 **Tilehurst 1.3miles (2.1km)**

S M T W T F S   S M T W T F S

In Post Office. Café at Mapledurham Lock, open daily in summer and weekends in winter

B&B Ivy Cottage

Mrs Rosalind Young
Purley Village, Reading RG8 8AF
T: 0118 984 4123 **M:** 07779 679552
E: rosalind@ivycottage-bandb.co.uk
www. ivycottage-bandb.co.uk
🛏 1 £80 🛏 1 £80 (£55) ⚔ V ♦ O
DRY 🔲 🚗 ⚹ 📶 One room en-suite
♨ Lift provided to local pub/restaurant.

⚑ Mapledurham Lock

The Lock Keeper
Purley, Reading RG8 8BE
T: 0118 941 7776 www.environment-agency.gov.uk/homeandleisure
⚑ 5 £8 🔲 🔧 🔧 🖐 ♿WC 💳
Mastercard, Visa
♨ No vehicle access to site. Phone to book. Dogs must be kept on leads.

TILEHURST

⊕ **SU6674** 👢 **on path**
🚂 **Tilehurst**

Close to range of services in Reading.

18 Partridge Drive   **B&B**

Mr & Mrs Wyatt
Tilehurst RG31 4SX
T: 0118 962 5419 **M:** 07964 862038
E: veronicawyatt7@gmail.com
🛏 1 £50 (£30) 🛏 2 £30 ♦ O DRY
📶 ★★★

Firtrees   **B&B**

Mrs Joan Reed
2 Cotswold Way, Tilehurst RG31 6SH
T: 0118 941 3286 **M:** 07960 713184
E: joanreed@mail.com
🛏 1 £50 (£40) 🛏 2 £30 V 🎿 ♦ ♦
O DRY 🔲 ⚹ 📶 ★★
♨ Lift provided to local pub/restaurant.

Yellow flag iris

Section

Tilehurst to Henley-on-Thames

Once Reading is left behind this 12 miles (20km) section enjoys a landscape of gentle wooded hills, fine houses and, of course, the ever-widening River Thames. There are also several pleasant settlements en route for refreshments.

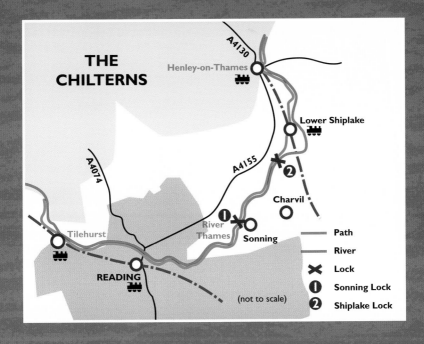

Maps

| Landranger maps | 175 | Reading & Windsor |
| Explorer maps | 171 | Chiltern Hills West |

Taxi Services

Place	Name	Telephone numbers
Reading	Berkshire Cars	0118 950 0400
	Premier Cars	0118 950 0500
	Thames Valley Taxis Ltd	0118 948 4848
	Theale Taxis	0118 930 2345
Sonning	Top Cars	0118 944 2222
Henley	Chiltern Taxis	01491 578899
	County Cars	01491 579696
	Harris Taxis	01491 577036

Car Parks

The following is a list of public car parks close to the Thames Path and does not include on-street parking in villages or towns. Where there are several car parks in a town, those closest to the Path have been listed. Unfortunately theft from vehicles parked in the countryside does occasionally occur, so please leave valuables you don't want to carry at home.

Place	Map Grid Reference
Reading, various including King's Meadow Road	
Henley-on-Thames, Mill Lane	SU 771817
Henley-on-Thames, Mill Meadows	SU 766822

Toilets ⊕ & ♿ and Water Points at Locks 🚰

Place	Map Grid Reference
Reading, various ⊕ ♿	
Sonning Lock ⊕	SU 753755
Shiplake Lock ⊕ 🚰	SU 776787
Henley-on-Thames, various inc Mill Meadows ⊕ ♿	SU 766822

Visitor Information Centres

* Offers accommodation booking service for personal callers during opening hours.

Place

Address/Opening Hours

*Henley-on-Thames

Henley Town Hall, Henley-on-Thames   RG9 2AQ
T: 01491 578034
E: vic@henleytowncouncil.co.uk
www.visitsouthoxfordshire.co.uk

Opening hours:
Oct-March: Mon-Sat 10:30-15:30
April-Sept: Mon-Sat 10:00-16:00

READING

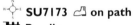 **SU7173** ⌐ **on path**

🚆 **Reading**

Large town with full range of services, visit www.livingreading.co.uk for further details. It has a wide range of accommodation.

SONNING

SU7675 ⌐ **on path**

🚆 **Twyford 2.8miles (4.5km)** ⓗ

S M T W T F S   S M T W T F S

S M T W T F S   S M T W T F S

In Bull Inn
Pubs: Bull Inn 0118 9693901 &
Great House 0118 969 2277

Bull Inn Hotel   ⓗ

Mrs Christine Mason
High Street, Sonning RG4 6UP
T: 0118 969 3901
E: thebullinn@fullers.co.uk
www.bullinnsonning.co.uk
🛏 6 £99 🛏 1 £150 ♨ V 🗴 🌑 🍎
📶 🆅🆂🅰 Most major cards ★★★★ All rooms en-suite.
🛎 VisitEngland Silver Award.

Great House at Sonning   ⓗ

Mrs Julie Rae
Thames Street, Sonning RG4 6UT
T: 0118 969 2277
E: enquiries@greathouseatsonning.co.uk
www.greathouseatsonning.co.uk
🛏 33 £119 🛏 8 £119 🛏 2 £134
🛏 3 £89 ♨ ♿ V 🌑 🍸 📶 🆅🆂🅰 Most major cards ★★★ All rooms en-suite
🛎 No evening meals on Sundays

CHARVIL

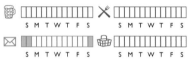 **SU7775** 1.3miles (2km)
Twyford 1.6miles (2.6km)PF

£ At the garage
Pubs: Lands End 0118 934 0700 &
Wee Waif 0118 9440066

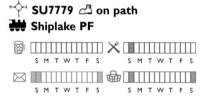 Wee Waif Lodge

Mr Brad House
Old Bath Road, Charvil RG10 9RJ
T: 0118 944 0066
E: 5306@greeneking.co.uk
www.hungryhorse.co.uk
42 £50 Most major cards ★★★All rooms
en-suite

LOWER SHIPLAKE

SU7779 on path
Shiplake PF

Pub: Baskerville Arms 0118 9403332.
For further information visit www.
shiplake.net

Baskerville   *Closed 25 & 31 Dec*

Mr Allan Hannah
Station Road, Lower Shiplake RG9 3NY
T: 0118 940 3332
E: enquiries@thebaskerville.com
www.thebaskerville.com
2 £99 1 £99 (£89) 1 £109
Most major cards, Paypal ★★★★ All rooms
en-suite.
VisitEngland Silver & Breakfast
awards. No evening meals on Sundays

Garden Room   B&B

Mrs Kay Landau
Ashburton House, Lashbrook Road,
Lower Shiplake, Henley RG9 3NX
T: 0118 940 2203 M: 07881 518780
E: steve.landau2@btinternet.com
www.shiplakebedandbreakfast.com
1 £65 (£55) Room is
en-suite

The Baskerville

★★★★

Station Road, Lower Shiplake,
Henley-on-Thames, RG9 3NY
Tel: 0118 940 3332
www.thebaskerville.com

The Baskerville is the perfect blend of traditional village pub,
superb restaurant and excellent accommodation.

The bar with its signed rugby shirts and sporting memorabilia has four
cask ales on tap and a choice of over 40 malt whiskies. The cuisine is
modern British with Continental and Eastern influence. Menus change
frequently to match the seasons. Dishes are cooked to order using
fresh, locally and organically sourced produce. To complement the
food is a wine list of over 50 bins.

'Pick of the Pubs' in AA Pub Guide. Child and pet friendly.

HENLEY-ON-THAMES

⊕ **SU7682** ◁ **on path**
🚆 **Henley-on-Thames**

Town with full range of services,
visit www.henley-on-thames.org for
further details. It has a wide range of
accommodation – details from Visitor
Information Centre (see section
introduction).

☆ River and Rowing Museum
T: 01491 415600   www.rrm.co.uk

☆ Hobbs of Henley - boat hire & trips
T: 01491 572035
www.hobbs-of-henley.com

Swiss Farm Touring and Camping   *Closed Nov-March*   ⛺ SC

Mr Joseph Borlase
Marlow Road, Henley RG9 2HY
T: 01491 573419
E: enquiries@swissfarmcamping.co.uk
www.swissfarmcamping.co.uk
⛺ 50 £14 🚐 134 £14 🚰 🚿 ⊕
♿WC 🔌 📷 📶 🏧 **CG** 💳 Most
major cards ★★★★★
🚍 Caravans for hire £290/week.

Henley-on-Thames

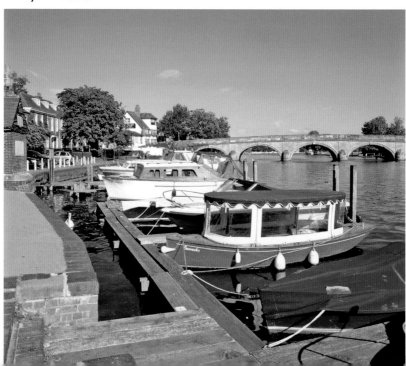

Section 9

Henley-on-Thames to Marlow

The pleasures of this 9 miles (14km) stretch of the Path lie in walking beside the now mature river surrounded by the wooded slopes of the Chiltern Hills. There are likely to be more people enjoying the Path and river than on previous sections but it's rarely very busy

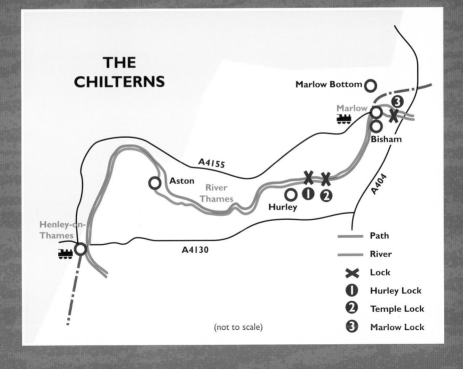

THE CHILTERNS

Marlow Bottom

Marlow

Bisham

Aston

River Thames

A4155

Hurley

A404

Henley-on-Thames

A4130

Path

River

Lock

❶ Hurley Lock

❷ Temple Lock

❸ Marlow Lock

(not to scale)

Maps

Landranger maps	175	Reading & Windsor
Explorer maps	171	Chiltern Hills West
	172	Chiltern Hills East

Taxi Services

Place	Name	Telephone numbers
Henley	Chiltern Taxis	01491 578899
	County Cars	01491 579696
	Harris Taxis	01491 577036
Marlow	Cresta Cars	01628 476395
	Marlow Express Cars	01628 487722

Car Parks

The following is a list of public car parks close to the Thames Path and does not include on-street parking in villages or towns. Where there are several car parks in a town, those closest to the Path have been listed. Unfortunately theft from vehicles parked in the countryside does occasionally occur, so please leave valuables you don't want to carry at home.

Place	Map Grid Reference
Henley-on-Thames, Mill Lane	SU 771817
Henley-on-Thames, Mill Meadows	SU 766822
Mill End, south of Hambleden off A4122 (cross the river via Hambleden weir)	SU 785855
Hurley	SU 825841
Marlow, Pound Lane	SU 849863
Marlow, Gossmore recreation grounds	SU 858861

Toilets (♿) & ♿ and Water Points at Locks 🚰

Place	Map Grid Reference
Henley-on-Thames, various inc Mill Meadows (♿) ♿	SU 766822
Mill End car park, south of Hambleden (cross the river via Hambleden weir) (♿) ♿	SU 785855
Hurley Lock (♿) ♿ 🚰	SU 826843
Temple Lock (♿) 🚰	SU 837844
Marlow, Higginson Park (♿) ♿	SU 850863
Marlow Lock (♿) 🚰	SU 855860

Visitor Information Centres

* Offers accommodation booking service for personal callers during opening hours.

Place	Address/Opening Hours
*Henley-on-Thames	Henley Town Hall, Henley-on-Thames RG9 2AQ **T**: 01491 578034 **E**: vic@henleytowncouncil.co.uk www.visitsouthoxfordshire.co.uk

Opening hours:
Oct-March: Mon-Sat 10:30-15:30
April-Sept: Mon-Sat 10:00-16:00

*Marlow — 55A High Street, Marlow SL7 1BA
T: 01628 483597 **E**: tourism_enquiries@wycombe.gov.uk
www.marlowtown.co.uk

Opening hours:
All year: Mon-Fri 9:00-17:00; Sat 9:30-17:00

From Temple Bridge

ASTON

⊕ **SU7884** 👢 **on path**
🚂 **Henley-on-Thames 2.8miles (4.5km)**

S M T W T F S   S M T W T F S

Pub: Flower Pot Hotel 01491 574721

INN | **Flowerpot Hotel**

Pat Thatcher & Tony Read
Ferry Lane, Aston RG9 3DG
T: 01491 574721 **E:** pt.pot@tiscali.co.uk
🛏 2 £120 💤 1 £60 (£60) 🚹 V 🏕
🌑 🍎 O **DRY** 🚗 🛜 📶 Most major cards. Double rooms en-suite
🏠 No evening meals on Sundays

HURLEY

⊕ **SU8285** 👢 **on path**
🚂 **Marlow 3.7miles (6km) P F**
⊕ 🚻 WC

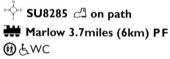
S M T W T F S   S M T W T F S

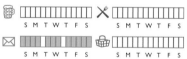
S M T W T F S   S M T W T F S

B&B | **Meadow View**

Ms Linda Proctor
Henley Road, Hurley SL6 5LW
T: 01628 829764 **M:** 07702 275612
E: lin.meadowview@tiscali.co.uk
www.meadowviewbedandbreakfast.co.uk
🛏 2 £80 🚹 (min age 12) V 🏕 🌑
🍽 O 📶 ★★★★★ One room en-suite
🏠 VisitEngland Silver Award.

Hurley Bed & Breakfast | **B&B**

Mrs Katie Gear
The Old Farm House, High Street,
Hurley SL6 5NB
T: 01628 825446
E: k.gear@btinternet.com
www.hurleybedandbreakfast.co.uk
🛏 3 £80 💤 2 £80 (£60) 🛏 3 £60
🚹 (min age 12) 📶 💳 Most major cards. All rooms en-suite
🏠 Minimum 2 nights stay

Hurley Riverside Park | **SC**
Closed 1 Nov-28 Feb

Mr Will Burfitt
Park Office, Hurley SL6 5NE
T: 01628 824493
E: info@hurleyriversidepark.co.uk
www.hurleyriversidepark.co.uk
⛺ 62 £13 🚐 138 £15 🔌 🚿 ♨ 🚻
♿WC 🖥 🧺 📻 CG 💳 Most major cards ★★★★
🏠 Self-catering accommodation available from £300 per week

Hurley Lock *Closed Oct-March* ⛺

The Lock Keeper
Mill Lane, Hurley SL6 5ND
T: 01628 824334 www.environment-agency.gov.uk/homeandleisure
⛺ 10 £8 🔌 🚿 ♨ 🚻 🖥 💳 Most major cards
🏠 Phone to book. Dogs must be kept on leads. No vehicle access. Refreshment kiosk April-September.

BISHAM

 SU8585 1.2miles (1.9km)
Marlow 1.4miles (2.2km)

S M T W T F S   S M T W T F S

Pub: Bull Inn 01628 484734

☆ Bisham Abbey National Sports
Centre - open to visitors
T: 01628 476911
www.bishamabbeynsc.co.uk

B&B Old Vicarage   *Closed Xmas & New Year*

Heather Oliver
Church Lane, Bisham SL7 1RW
T: 01628 474795
E: theoldvicaragebisham@gmail.com
www.theoldvicaragebisham.co.uk
 1 £110 **V**
Room is en-suite

MARLOW

 SU8586 on path
Marlow

Town with full range of services,
visit www.marlowtown.co.uk for
further details. It has a wide range of
accommodation – details from Visitor
Information Centre (see section
introduction).

Longridge Activity Centre
SC

Bookings Team
Quarry Wood Road, Marlow SL7 1RE
T: 01628 483252
E: bookings@longridge.org.uk
www.longridge-uk.org
350 people £5/person
WC Most major cards
and Paypal
Book in advance. Also dormitory
accommodation for 83 from £10/person
without breakfast but self-catering
kitchen available. On-site café open from
10:00 to 17:30 during summer which
can provide meals later if pre-booked

MARLOW BOTTOM

 SU8488 1.9miles (3km)
Marlow 2.2miles (3.5km)

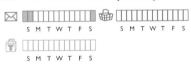
S M T W T F S   S M T W T F S
S M T W T F S

☆ Rebellion Brewery Tours
T: 01628 476594

Sue Simmons Bed & Breakfast   **B&B**

Mrs Sue Simmons
61 Hill Farm Road, Marlow Bottom
SL7 3LX
T: 01628 475145 **M:** 07502 356017
E: suesimmons@
accommodationmarlow.com
www.accommodationmarlow.com
1 £90 (£60) 2 £40 (Min age
5) **V** ★★
VisitEngland Silver Award. Double/
twin occupancy of family room £60

Section 10

Marlow to Windsor

This 14 miles (22km) section travels through particularly attractive wooded countryside as far as Maidenhead. Beyond Maidenhead the river becomes busier and in places there are views of grand homes finishing with the grandest of them all, Windsor Castle, towering above the water.

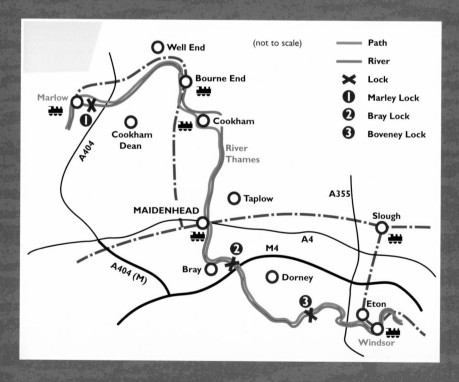

(not to scale)

Path

River

✖ **Lock**

❶ **Marley Lock**

❷ **Bray Lock**

❸ **Boveney Lock**

Well End

Bourne End

Marlow

❶ Cookham

Cookham Dean

Cookham

River Thames

Taplow

A355

MAIDENHEAD

Slough

A4

❷ M4

A404 (M)

Bray

Dorney

❸

Eton

Windsor

Maps

Landranger maps	175	Reading & Windsor
Explorer maps	172	Chiltern Hills East
	160	Windsor, Weybridge & Bracknell

Taxi Services

Place	Name	Telephone numbers
Marlow	Cresta Cars	01628 476395
	Marlow Express Cars	01628 487722
Bourne End	Bourne End Cars	01628 523232
	Central Cars	01494 462232
Maidenhead	A-Z Cars	01628 621234
	Best Way Taxis	01628 777585
	Dial-a-car	01628 780052
	Dot 2 Dot	01628 200999
	Maidenhead Taxi Rank	01628 634311
Windsor	Dot 2 Dot	01753 842020
	Five Star Car Hire	01753 859555 or 858888
	Windsor Cabs	01753 585585
	Windsor Cars	01753 677677

Car Parks

The following is a list of public car parks close to the Thames Path and does not include on-street parking in villages or towns. Where there are several car parks in a town, those closest to the Path have been listed. Unfortunately theft from vehicles parked in the countryside does occasionally occur, so please leave valuables you don't want to carry at home.

Place	Map Grid Reference
Marlow, Pound Lane	SU 849863
Marlow, Gossmore recreation grounds	SU 858861
Spade Oak, west of Bourne End	SU 884876
Bourne End, Wakeman Road	SU 895874
Cookham, Sutton Road	SU 897853
Maidenhead, Boulters Lock, Lower Cookham Road	SU 902825
Boveney	SU 938777
Eton, Meadow Lane	SU 965773
Windsor, River Street	SU 967771

Toilets (♿) & and Water Points at Locks

Place	Map Grid Reference
Marlow, Higginson Park	SU 850863
Marlow Lock	SU 855860
Bourne End, Wakeman Road car park	SU 895874
Cookham, Sutton Road car park	SU 897853
Maidenhead, various inc Ray Mill Island	SU 903826
Bray Lock	SU 798910
Boveney Lock	SU 778945
Eton Court Car Park	SU 967774
Windsor, various inc Windsor & Eton Riverside Station	

Visitor Information Centres

* Offers accommodation booking service for personal callers during opening hours.

Place	Address/Opening Hours
*Marlow	55A High Street, Marlow SL7 1BA **T**: 01628 483597 **E**: tourism_enquiries@wycombe.gov.uk www.marlowtown.co.uk **Opening hours:** All year: Mon-Fri 9:00-17:00; Sat 9:30-17:00
*Maidenhead	The Library, St Ives Road, Maidenhead SL6 1QU **T**: 01628 796502 **E**: maidenhead.tic@rbwm.gov.uk www.windsor.gov.uk **Opening hours:** All year: Mon/Wed 09:30-17:00; Tues/Thurs 09:30-20:00; Fri 09:30-19:00; Sat 09:30-16:00
*Windsor	Old Booking Hall, Windsor Royal Shopping, Thames Street, Windsor SL4 1PJ **T**: 01753 743900 **E**: windsor.tic@rbwm.gov.uk www.windsor.gov.uk **Opening hours:** April-May: Mon-Sat 10:00-17:00; Sun 10:00-16:00 June-Oct: Mon-Fri 9:30-17:30; Sat 9:30-17:00; Sun 10:00-16:00 Nov-Mar: Sun-Fri 10:00-16:00; Sat 10:00-17:00

COOKHAM DEAN

⊕ **SU8785** 2 miles (3.2km)
🚂 **Cookham Rise 1.4miles (2.2km)**

🍺 ⦚⦚⦚⦚⦚⦚⦚⦚⦚⦚⦚ ✕ ⦚⦚⦚⦚⦚⦚⦚⦚⦚⦚⦚
　　S M T W T F S 　　　S M T W T F S

For further information visit
www.cookham.com

Ⓗ Sanctum on the Green

Mr Colin Rooney
Old Cricket Common, Cookham Dean
SL6 9NZ
T: 01628 482638 **F:** 01628 487474
E: info@sanctumonthegreen.com
www.sanctumonthegreen.com
🛏 9 £135 ⚥ 📺 V 🏍 🌳 🌑 ● 🔘 👣
📶 💳 All major cards ★★★★ All
rooms en-suite.

B&B Cartlands Cottage

Mrs Tessa Parkes
Kings Lane, Cookham Dean SL6 9AY
T: 01628 482196
🛏 1 £70 (£45) ⚥ V ● O 🚗 👣
📶 Room is en-suite.
🛗 Lift provided to local pub.

WELL END

⊕ **SU8887** 0.2miles (0.4km)
🚂 **Bourne End 0.8miles (1.2km)**

🍺 ⦚⦚⦚⦚⦚⦚⦚⦚⦚⦚⦚ ✕ ⦚⦚⦚⦚⦚⦚⦚⦚⦚⦚⦚
　　S M T W T F S 　　　S M T W T F S

Pub: Spade Oak 01628 520090

☆ Spade Oak Lake Nature Reserve

BOURNE END

⊕ **SU8987** on path
🚂 **Bourne End**

Small town with range of services

COOKHAM

⊕ **SU8985** on path
🚂 **Cookham Rise 1mile (1.6km)**
P F Ⓦ ♿WC

🍺 ⦚⦚⦚⦚⦚⦚⦚⦚⦚⦚⦚ ✕ ⦚⦚⦚⦚⦚⦚⦚⦚⦚⦚⦚
　　S M T W T F S 　　　S M T W T F S
🍽 ⦚⦚⦚⦚⦚⦚⦚⦚⦚⦚⦚ 🎁 ⦚⦚⦚⦚⦚⦚⦚⦚⦚⦚⦚
　　S M T W T F S 　　　S M T W T F S
☕ ⦚⦚⦚⦚⦚⦚⦚⦚⦚⦚⦚
　　S M T W T F S

Small convenience store at garage.

☆ Stanley Spencer Gallery
T: 01628 471885
www.stanleyspencer.org.uk

Cookham Lock　　*Closed Oct-March* ⛺

The Lock Keeper
Odney Lane, Cookham SL6 9SR
T: 01628 520752 www.environment-
agency.gov.uk/homeandleisure
⛺ 10 £5.50 📷 🔥 🔥 Ⓦ 📄
🛗 Phone to book. Dogs must be
kept on leads. No vehicle access.
Refreshment kiosk Easter-September,
weekends and school holidays.

B&B | **Swiss Bed and Breakfast**

Mrs Susanne Wilkinson
Uf Dorf, Terry's Lane, Cookham SL6 9RT
M: 07758 505014
E: fmikewilkinson@gmail.com
www.swissbedandbreakfast.co.uk

🛏 2 £65 (£50) 🛏 1 £40 � V🔥
● ● DRY 🔲 🚗 ⬚ ⏰ Double rooms en-suite

🛏 Single room has private bathroom. Lift provided to local pub/restaurant.

MAIDENHEAD

⌖ **SU8981** 👢 **on path**
🚌 **Maidenhead Central**

Town with full range of services, visit www.maidenhead.net for further details. It has a wide range of accommodation – details from Visitor Information Centre (see section introduction).

TAPLOW

⌖ **SU9082** 👢 **1.1mile (1.8km)**
🚌 **Taplow 0.8miles (1.2km)**

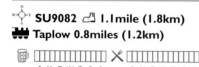

| 🍺 | S M T W T F S | ✕ | S M T W T F S |
| ☕ | S M T W T F S | | |

☆ Cliveden - National Trust property overlooking the Thames
T: 01628 668561
www.nationaltrust.org.uk/cliveden

Cliveden 🏠

Taplow SL6 0JF
T: 01628 668561
E: reservations@clivedenhouse.co.uk
www.clivedenhouse.co.uk

🛏 38 £252 � ♿ 🔲 V 🔥 ◐ i O
DRY 🔲 🚗 👣 ⏰
💳 All major cards ★★★★★ All rooms en-suite

Amerden Caravan & Camping Park *Closed Nov-March* ⛺

Mrs Beverley Hakesley
Amerden Lane, Taplow SL6 0EE
T: 01628 627461
E: beverly@amerdencaravanpark.co.uk
www.amerdencaravanpark.webs.com

⛺ 30 £12 🚐 30 £23 🔲 🔥 🔲 👤
♿WC 🔲 🔲 ⏰

Bridge Cottage Guest House *Closed Xmas-14 Jan* **B&B**

Mrs A Staszewski
Bath Road, Taplow SL6 0AR
T: 01628 626805
www.bridgecottagebb.co.uk

🛏 2 £59 (£50) 🛏 2 £64 🛏 2 £39
� ♿ V ● O DRY ⏰ ★★★ Some rooms en-suite

Amerden Lodge **B&B**

Mr Nigel Saw
Old Marsh Lane, Taplow SL6 0EE
T: 01628 673458 **M:** 07780 976665
E: nigel.saw@btinternet.com

🛏 1 £65 🛏 1 £65 (£40) � 🔲 V
🔥 ◐ i O DRY 🔲 🚗 👣 ⏰ Some rooms en-suite or private bathroom

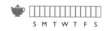

BRAY

⊹ SU9079 1.3miles (2km)
Maidenhead Central 1.6miles
(2.5km) PF ⓗ ♿WC

S M T W T F S   S M T W T F S

S M T W T F S

B&B **Old Coach House**

Mrs Fiona Stewart
3 Windsor Road, Braywick, Maidenhead
SL6 1UZ
T: 01628 671244
E: theoldcoachhouse3@btinternet.com
www.oldcoachhouse.biz
🛏 1 £60 🛏 2 £60 (£40) 🛏 1 £100
🛏 1 £40 ♟ (min age 5) 🖼 V DRY ⊡
📶 Some rooms en-suite

DORNEY & DORNEY REACH

⊹ SU9379 0.9miles (1.5km)
Taplow 1.7miles (2.7km)PF

S M T W T F S   S M T W T F S

S M T W T F S

Pubs: Pineapple 01628 662353
(sandwich menu only) &
Palmer Arms 01628 666612

☆ Dorney Court
T: 01628 604638
www.dorneycourt.co.uk

☆ Jubilee River with various
recreational opportunities

ETON

⊹ SU9677 on path
Windsor & Eton Riverside
0.3miles (0.5km)

Small town with a range of services,
visit www.eton.co.uk for further details.

The Christopher Ⓗ

Mrs Janet Trewrtha
110 High Street, Eton SL4 6AN
T: 01753 852359
E: reservations@thechristopher.co.uk
www.thechristopher.co.uk
🛏 35 £130 🛏 9 £100 ♟ ♿ 🖼
V 🅰 🌑 ● ○ DRY ⊡ 🐾 📶 VISA All
major cards ★★★ All rooms en-suite

WINDSOR

⊹ SU9676 on path
Windsor Central

Town with full range of services, visit
www.windsor.gov.uk for further details.
It has a wide range of accommodation
– details from Visitor Information
Centre (see section introduction).

☆ Windsor Castle
T: 020 7766 7300
www.royalcollection.org.uk

☆ LEGOLAND® Windsor
T: 0871 222 2001
www.legoland.co.uk

☆ Savill Garden
T: 01784 435544
www.theroyallandscape.co.uk

Suspension bridge at Marlow

Near Bray Lock

Section 11

Windsor to Shepperton

As the Thames Path gets closer to London the number of riverside settlements inevitably increase, but along this 14 miles (22km) section there are still considerable amounts of green space to enjoy before reaching Shepperton.

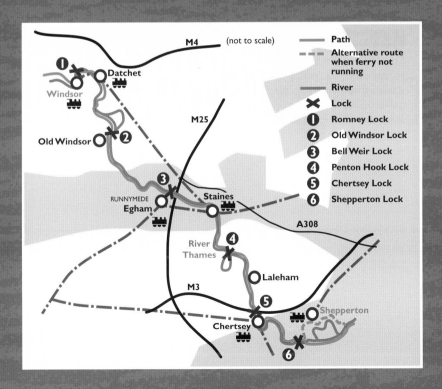

—	Path
- - -	Alternative route when ferry not running
—	River
✕	Lock
❶	Romney Lock
❷	Old Windsor Lock
❸	Bell Weir Lock
❹	Penton Hook Lock
❺	Chertsey Lock
❻	Shepperton Lock

M4 (not to scale)

Datchet

Windsor

M25

Old Windsor

RUNNYMEDE
Egham

Staines

A308

River
Thames

Laleham

M3

Chertsey

Shepperton

Maps

Landranger maps	175	Reading & Windsor
	176	West London
Explorer maps	160	Windsor, Weybridge & Bracknell

Taxi Services

Place	Name	Telephone numbers
Windsor	Dot 2 Dot	01753 842020
	Five Star Car Hire	01753 859555 or 858888
	Windsor Cabs	01753 585585
	Windsor Cars	01753 677677
Egham	Arrow Cars	01784 436533
	Egham Taxis	01784 433933
	Gemini Cars	01784 471111
Chertsey	A & C Cars	01932 570170

Car Parks

The following is a list of public car parks close to the Thames Path and does not include on-street parking in villages or towns. Where there are several car parks in a town, those closest to the Path have been listed. Unfortunately theft from vehicles parked in the countryside does occasionally occur, so please leave valuables you don't want to carry at home.

Place	Map Grid Reference
Windsor, River Street	SU 967771
Romney Lock	SU 970776
Windsor Home Park	SU 970777
Runnymede National Trust (April to end September)	SU 995733
Runnymede Pleasure Grounds	TQ 007724
Staines, Bridge Street	TQ 032716
Laleham	TQ 051686
Laleham Park, Thameside	TQ 053677
Chertsey Bridge	TQ 055666
Shepperton Lock	TQ 072660

Toilets ⓦ & ♿ and Water Points at Locks 🚰

Place	Map Grid Reference
Windsor, various inc Windsor & Eton Riverside Station ⓦ ♿	SU 968773
Romney Lock ⓦ 🚰	SU 970776
Old Windsor Lock ⓦ 🚰	SU 995747
Runnymede Pleasure Grounds ⓦ ♿	TQ 007724
Bell Weir Lock ⓦ	TQ 017721
Staines, various inc Thames Street ⓦ ♿	TQ 036714
Penton Hook Lock ⓦ 🚰	TQ 044695
Laleham Park, Thameside ⓦ ♿	TQ 053677
Chertsey Lock 🚰	TQ 054668
Shepperton Lock ⓦ ♿ 🚰	TQ 072660

Visitor Information Centres

* Offers accommodation booking service for personal callers during opening hours.

Place

*Windsor

Address/Opening Hours

Old Booking Hall, Windsor Royal Shopping, Thames Street, Windsor SL4 1PJ
T: 01753 743900
E: windsor.tic@rbwm.gov.uk   www.windsor.gov.uk

Opening hours:
April-May: Mon-Sat 10:00-17:00; Sun 10:00-16:00

June-Oct: Mon-Fri 9:30-17:30; Sat 9:30-17:00; Sun 10:00-16:00

Nov-Mar: Sun-Fri 10:00-16:00; Sat 10:00-17:00

Windsor Castle

95

DATCHET

 **SU9876** 🥾 **on path**
🚉 **Datchet**
Small town with range of services, visit
www.datchet.com for further details

B&B 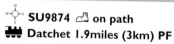 **Lowlands Guest House**   *closed Dec*

Mr Mike Donnelly
137 Slough Road, Datchet SL3 9AE
T: 01753 591388 **M:** 07789 147157
E: mike@bridgelock.com
www.datchet.com
🛏 2 £65 🛏 2 £80 🛏 1 £60 ⛼
V🛁🍴 O 🚗 🛜 💳 Paypal. Some
rooms en-suite.

OLD WINDSOR

 **SU9874** 🥾 **on path**
🚉 **Datchet 1.9miles (3km) PF**

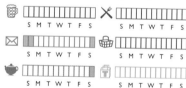

🅿 In Co-op

INN  **Union Inn**

Mr Almond
17 Crimp Hill, Old Windsor SL4 2QY
T: 01753 861955
🛏 8 £75 (£65) 🛏 4 £60 ⛼ 🖼 V 🌓
🍴🛜 💳 Most major cards ★★★★
All rooms en-suite.

EGHAM

 **TO0171** 🥾 **on path**
🚉 **Egham 0.7miles (1.2km)**

Small town with a range of services, but
the accommodation below particularly
welcomes Thames Path walkers.
Visit www.egham.org.uk for further
details.

 **The Runnymede-on-Thames**

Windsor Road, Egham TW20 0AG
T: 01784 220600
E: info@therunnymede.co.uk
www.runnymedehotel.com
🛏 170 £169 🛏 38 £195 (£136)
🛏 28 £248 🛏 11 £132 ⛼ ♿V 🛁 🌓
🍴 O DRY 🍽 🚗 ⛼ 🛜 💳 All major
cards ★★★★ All rooms en-suite
H VisitEngland Silver & Breakfast
awards.

Beauvilla   *Closed Xmas to New Year*   B&B

Mrs Jo Wilding
44 Grange Road, Egham TW20 9QP
T: 01784 435115 **M:** 07793 555255
🛏 1 £55 🛏 1 £55 (£50) 🛏 2 £35
🖼 V 🍴 O DRY 🛜 Some rooms en-suite

STAINES

 **TO0371** 🥾 **on path**
🚉 **Staines**

Town with wide range of services and
accommodation

the perfect rest stop...

The runnymede-on-thames is located right beside Bell Weir lock between Windsor and Staines.

We offer the perfect riverside rest stop; whether you are taking a well earned overnight break in our comfy beds, refuelling with lunch in one of our two riverside restaurants, indulging in an afternoon tea or even just stopping for a refreshing drink in the lounge, you will receive a very warm welcome.

Call us for a chat on: 01784 220600 or visit www.therunnymede.co.uk

the runnymede-on-thames
hotel and spa

Windsor Road Egham Surrey TW20 0AG telephone: 01784 220600
email: info@therunnymede.co.uk www.therunnymede.co.uk

LALEHAM

TQ0568 🥾 on path
🚉 Staines 2.1miles (3.4km) PF

🍺 ▯▯▯▯▯▯▯▯▯▯ ✕ ▯▯▯▯▯▯▯▯▯▯
S M T W T F S   S M T W T F S

⊼ Laleham Park Campsite
Closed Oct-Mar

The Warden
Laleham Park, Thameside, Chertsey
TW18 1SS
T: 01932 564149
www.laleham.campingclub.co.uk
⊼/🚐 180 £12 🔌 🚿 🚰 ⓦ ♿WC
🔋 DRY 🔘 VISA Most major cards
🚹 Prices per person, children reduced
rate. Additional hook-up fee for
caravans.

CHERTSEY

TQ0466 🥾 on path
🚉 Chertsey 1.2miles (2km) PF

Small town with range of services, visit
www.chertsey.org.uk for further details

☆ Chertsey Musem
www.chertseymuseum.org.uk

Chertsey Camping & Caravanning Club ⊼

The Manager
Bridge Road, Chertsey KT16 8JX
T: 01932 562405
www.campingandcaravanningclub.co.uk/
chertsey
⊼/🚐 200 £8 🔌 🚿 🚰 ⓦ ♿WC 🔋
🔘 📷 CG 📶 VISA Most major cards
🚹 Prices per person, children reduced
rate.

SHEPPERTON

TQ0867 🥾 on path
🚉 Shepperton

Town with a full range of services, but
the accommodation below particularly
welcomes Thames Path walkers. For
information see www.shepperton-info.
co.uk

Splash Cottage B&B

Mr Malcolm Shaw
91 Watersplash Road, Shepperton
TW17 0EE
T: 01932 229987
E: info@lazy-river.co.uk
www.lazy-river.co.uk
🛏 1 £55 🛏 1 £55 (£35) 🛏 1 £35
👫 (min age 11) V 🐾 DRY 📶

Section 12

Shepperton to Teddington

This section is remarkably varied and includes vast reservoirs, an old racecourse, a royal palace and smart Kingston. It is the last non-tidal stretch of the Path as beyond Teddington Lock the River Thames is tidal.

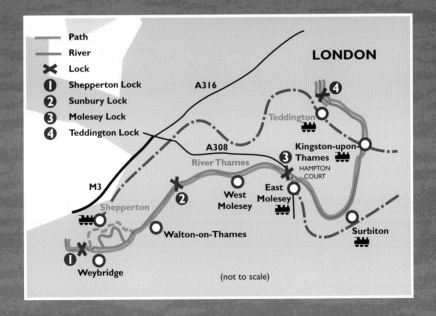

Legend:
- Path
- River
- ✖ Lock
- ❶ Shepperton Lock
- ❷ Sunbury Lock
- ❸ Molesey Lock
- ❹ Teddington Lock

LONDON

A316

Teddington

A308

River Thames

Kingston-upon-Thames

HAMPTON COURT

M3

West Molesey

East Molesey

Shepperton

Walton-on-Thames

Surbiton

❶ ✖ Weybridge

(not to scale)

Maps

Landranger maps	176	West London
Explorer maps	160	Windsor, Weybridge & Bracknell
	161	London South

Taxi Services

Place	Name	Telephone numbers
Weybridge	AGM Cars	01932 858585
	Eden Cars	01932 830830
Walton-on-Thames	Walton Station Taxis	01932 221484
	Swan Cars	01932 230830
East Molesey	Claremont Cars	020 8979 8866

Car Parks

The following is a list of public car parks close to the Thames Path and does not include on-street parking in villages or towns. Where there are several car parks in a town, those closest to the Path have been listed. Unfortunately theft from vehicles parked in the countryside does occasionally occur, so please leave valuables you don't want to carry at home.

Place	Map Grid Reference
Shepperton Lock	TQ 072660
Walton Bridge	TQ 094664
Molesey, Hurst Park	TQ 143693
Hampton Wick, by Kingston Bridge	TQ 176695
Kingston-upon-Thames, various	

Toilets ⊛ & ♿ and Water Points at Locks ⌖

Place	Map Grid Reference
Shepperton Lock ⊛ ♿ ⌖	TQ 072660
Walton Bridge ⊛ ♿	TQ 094664
Sunbury Lock ⊛ ♿ ⌖	TQ 109685
Molesey Lock ⊛ ⌖	TQ 153686
Kingston-upon-Thames, various ⊛ ♿	
Teddington Lock ⊛ ⌖	TQ 166716

Visitor Information Centres

* Offers accommodation booking service for personal callers during opening hours.

Place	Address/Opening Hours
Kingston-upon-Thames	Market House, Market Place, Kingston upon Thames KT1 1JS **T**: 020 8546 1140 www.kingston.gov.uk/browse/leisure/tourism

Opening hours:
All year: Mon 10:00-17:00; Wed to Sat 10:00-17:00;
Sun 11:00-17:00

WEYBRIDGE

✦ **TQ0764** 👢 **on path**
🚋 **Weybridge 1.2miles (2km)**

Town with a full range of services.
See www.allaboutweybridge.co.uk for
information

WALTON-ON-THAMES

✦ **TQ1066** 👢 **on path**
🚋 **Walton-on-Thames**

Town with a full range of services, but
the accommodation below particularly
welcomes Thames Path walkers.
See www.walton-on-thames.org for
information

The Cottage   B&B

Mrs Pat Sims
52 Bridge Street, Walton-on-Thames
KT12 1AP
T: 01932 242576 **E**: enquiries@
thecottagewaltononthames.co.uk
🛏 1 £75 🛏 1 £65 (£50) 🛏 1 £45
V ● O **DRY** 📶 Some rooms en-suite.

SURBITON

✦ **TQ1867** 👢 **1.3miles (2km)**
🚋

Town with a full range of services, but
the accommodation below particularly
welcomes Thames Path walkers. See
www.surbiton.com for information

⌂ Ditton Lodge

Mrs Roz Malakouti
47 Lovelace Road, Long Ditton KT6 6NZ
T: 020 8399 7482
E: info@dittonlodge.co.uk
www.dittonlodge.co.uk
🛏 14 £95 🛏 5 £95 (£85) 🛏 2
£115 🛏 2 £80 ⚡ V ◖ O ▣ 📶 VISA
All major cards ★★★★
All rooms en-suite.

B&B 21 Cotterill Road

Mrs Jennifer Booth
21 Cotterill Road, Surbiton KT6 7UW
M: 07971 670484
E: jenniferbooth@hotmail.co.uk
🛏 1 £50 🛏 1 £50 🛏 1 £25 V 📶

KINGSTON-UPON-THAMES

⊕ **TQ1869** 👢 **on path**
🚂 **Kingston-upon-Thames**

Outer London - full range of services available. Kingston has a wide range of accommodation, details from Visitor Information Centre (see section introduction)

TEDDINGTON

⊕ **TQ1671** 👢 **on path**
🚂 **Teddington**

Outer London - full range of services available. Contact Kingston Visitor Information Centre for further information (see section introduction)

View from Teddington footbridge

Section 13

LONDON: Teddington to Putney

From Teddington the Thames Path offers a choice of walking routes either side of the river as far as Island Gardens on the Isle of Dogs. The south bank along this section (12 miles/19km) has a surprisingly rural feel, and the north bank (14 miles/23km) too has several lengthy green stretches. Whichever route is taken, there's an enormous amount to see and visit.

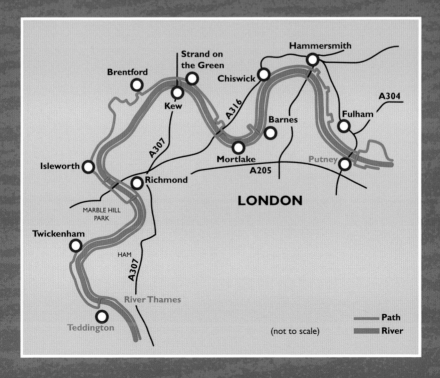

Maps

Landranger maps	176	West London
Explorer maps	161	London South

Car Parks

Between Teddington and Putney there are a number of parking opportunities. Walkers are advised not to use their cars if at all possible - public transport is widely available and there is also a congestion charge which is now in force for those who drive into central London.

Visitor Information Centres

* Offers accommodation booking service for personal callers during opening hours.

Place	Address/Opening Hours
Hammersmith	20 Broadway Shopping Centre, Queen Caroline Street, Hammersmith W6 **T**: 020 8748 3079 www.visithammersmith.co.uk **Opening hours:** All year: Mon-Fri 11:00-18:00

Hammersmith

Section 14

LONDON: Putney to Tower Bridge

This is a relatively short section (11 miles/17km along the south bank and 10 miles/16km on the north bank) but one packed with the fascinating history of London. Virtually the whole of the route is built up but there is a range of old and modern architecture to enjoy and the odd patch of green to sit in and to enjoy the river.

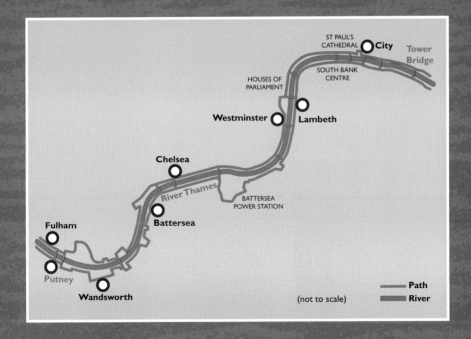

Maps

Landranger maps	176	West London
Explorer maps	161	London South
	173	London North

Car Parks

Between Putney and Tower Bridge there are a number of parking opportunities. Walkers are advised not to use their cars if at all possible - public transport is widely available and there is also a congestion charge which is now in force for those who drive into central London.

Visitor Information Centres

* Offers accommodation booking service for personal callers during opening hours.

Place	Address/Opening Hours
*Britain and London Visitor Centre	1 Regent Street, London SW1Y 4XT
	www.visitlondon.com
	Opening hours:
	All Year: Mon-Fri 9:30-18:00; Sat & Sun 10:00-16:00
*City of London	St Paul's Churchyard, EC4M 8BX
	www.visitthecity.co.uk
	Opening hours:
	All year: Mon-Sat 9:30-17:30
	Sun 10:00-16:00

Peace Pagoda in Battersea Park

106

TEDDINGTON TO PUTNEY

Full range of services and accommodation available. Visit www.visitlondon.com for further information

PUTNEY TO TOWER BRIDGE

Full range of services and accommodation available. Visit www.visitlondon.com for further information

▲ Earl's Court YHA

38 Bolton Gardens, Earl's Court SW5 0AQ
T: 0845 371 9114
E: earlscourt@yha.org.uk
www.yha.org.uk
♯♦ 🚯 🗟 📼 Most major cards
🛏 Rooms from £40, beds from £16/ adult. Luggage storage.

▲ Holland Park YHA

Holland Walk, Kensington W8 7QU
T: 0845 371 9122
E: hollandpark@yha.org.uk
www.yha.org.uk
♯♦ V 🚲 🚯 🗟 📼 Most major cards
🛏 Rooms £31, beds from £13/adult. Luggage storage.

Oxford Street YHA ▲

14 Noel Street W1F 8GF
T: 0845 371 9133
E: oxfordst@yha.org.uk
www.yha.org.uk
♯♦(min age 12) 🗟 📶 📼 Most major cards
🛏 Rooms from £47, beds from £19/ adult. Luggage storage. Self catering only.

London Central YHA ▲

104 Bolsover Street W1W 5NU
T: 0845 371 9154
E: londoncentral@yha.org.uk
www.yha.org.uk
♯♦ ♿ 🚲 🚯 🗟 📼 Most major cards
Some rooms en-suite
🛏 Rooms from £38, beds from £15/ adult. Luggage storage.

St Pancras YHA ▲

79-81 Euston Road NW1 2QE
T: 0845 371 9344
E: stpancras@yha.org.uk
www.yha.org.uk
♯♦ V 🚲 🚯 🗟 📼 Most major cards
Some rooms en-suite.
🛏 Rooms from £50 beds from £16/ adult. Luggage storage.

St Paul's YHA ▲

36 Carter Lane EC4V 5AB
T: 0845 371 9012
E: stpauls@yha.org.uk
www.yha.org.uk
♯♦ V 🚯 🗟 📼 Most major cards
🛏 Rooms from £30, beds from £13/adult

Section

15

LONDON: Tower Bridge to Thames Barrier

The Thames Path offers a choice of walking routes either side of the river along this section as far as Island Gardens on the Isle of Dogs opposite Greenwich (10 miles/16km on the south bank and 5miles/9km along the north bank). This is a section of old and new with some hidden corners still to find where it's possible to imagine what it was like when London was the busiest port in the world.

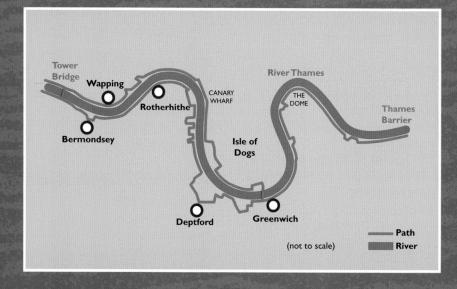

Tower Bridge

Wapping

Rotherhithe

CANARY WHARF

River Thames

THE DOME

Thames Barrier

Bermondsey

Isle of Dogs

Deptford

Greenwich

(not to scale)

— Path
— River

Maps

Landranger maps	177	East London
Explorer maps	173	London North
	162	Greenwich & Gravesend

Car Parks

Between Tower Bridge and the Thames Barrier there are a number of parking opportunities. Walkers are advised not to use their cars if at all possible - public transport is widely available and there is also a congestion charge which is now in force for those who drive into central London.

Visitor Information Centres

* Offers accommodation booking service for personal callers during opening hours.

Place | **Address/Opening Hours**

*City of London — St Paul's Churchyard, EC4M 8BX
www.visitthecity.co.uk

Opening hours:
All year: Mon-Sat 9:30-17:30
Sun 10:00-16:00

*Greenwich — Pepys House, 2 Cutty Sark Gardens, Greenwich, SE10 9LW
T: 0870 608 2000
www.visitgreenwich.org.uk

Opening hours:
All year: Daily 10:00-17:00
but closed 25th & 26th Dec

TOWER BRIDGE TO THAMES BARRIER

Full range of services and accommodation available. Visit www.visitlondon.com for further information

Thameside YHA ▲

20 Salter Rd, Rotherhithe SE16 5PR
T: 0845 371 9756
E: thameside@yha.org.uk
www.yha.org.uk
☼ V ⚲ Ⓝ ▢ 𝗩𝗜𝗦𝗔 Most major cards
Some rooms en-suite.
Ⓗ Rooms from £28, beds from £13/ adult

Tower Bridge

Canary Wharf from Greenland Dock